THE CREATIVE COOK

Savory to Sweet

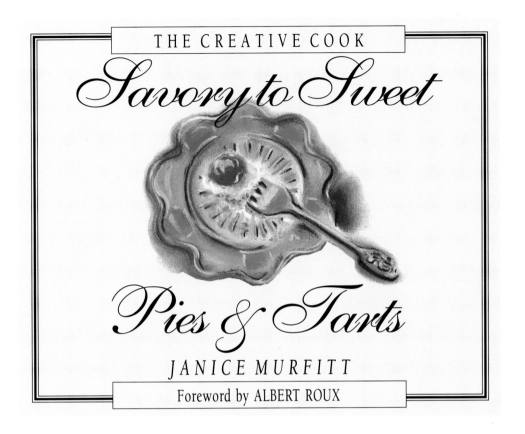

Pies & Tarts

JANICE MURFITT

Foreword by ALBERT ROUX

COLE
GROUP

*To Richard, Emma, and Anna for all their help
and support and for tasting all the recipes.*

Please note the following:

Quantities given in all the recipes serve 4 people unless otherwise stated.

Butter and margarine are packaged in a variety of forms, including 1-pound blocks and ¼-pound sticks. A stick equals 8 tablespoons (½ cup).

Cream used is specified as light cream (containing from 18 percent to 30 percent milk fat), whipping cream (30 percent to 36 percent milk fat), or heavy cream (at least 36 percent milk fat).

Flour used is all-purpose flour, unless otherwise specified.

Preparation of ingredients, such as the cleaning, trimming, and peeling of vegetables and fruit, is presumed and the text refers to any aspect of this only if unusual, such as onions used unpeeled, etc.

Citrus fruit should be thoroughly washed to remove any agricultural residues. For this reason, whenever a recipe uses the rind of any citrus such as oranges, lemon, or limes, the text specifies washed fruit. Wash the fruit thoroughly, rinse well, and pat dry. If using organically grown fruit, rinse briefly and pat dry.

Eggs used are large unless otherwise specified. Because of the risk of contamination with salmonella bacteria, current recommendations from health professionals are that children, pregnant women, people on immuno-suppressant drugs, and the elderly should not eat raw or lightly cooked eggs. This book includes recipes with raw and lightly cooked eggs. These recipes are marked by an ★ in the text.

Editorial Direction: Lewis Esson Publishing
Art Director: Mary Evans
Design: Sue Storey
Illustrations: Alison Barratt
Food for Photography: Janice Murfitt
Styling: Róisín Nield
Editorial Assistant: Penny David
American Editor: Norma MacMillan
Production: Julia Golding

Published by Cole Group
4415 Sonoma Highway/PO Box 4089
Santa Rosa, CA 95402–4089
(707) 538–0492   FAX (707) 538–0497

First published in 1992 by
Conran Octopus Limited,
37 Shelton Street, London WC2H 9HN

A   B   C   D   E   F   G   H
3   4   5   6   7   8   9   0

ISBN 1–56426–651–6
Library of Congress Cataloguing in process

Typeset by Servis Filmsetting Ltd
Printed and bound in Hong Kong

Distributed to the book trade by Publishers Group West

CONTENTS

FOREWORD

For someone like me, dedicated to good food, the concept of the tart conjures up nostalgic images of homemade strawberry jam, molasses, sliced apples, fresh nuts, egg and ham, prime mincemeat, and so on. Since my youth, a good tart with a thin, crisp pastry base and rich, flavorsome filling has always been high on my list of favorite foods. This may, of course, be one of the reasons that I chose to start my career as a chef by training as an apprentice *pâtissier*, or pastry chef.

These new books in the *Creative Cook* series are among the most exciting cookbooks I have seen in a long while. They reflect in a timely manner the full effects of the recent welcome change in the eating habits of many people in this country – as well as being healthier they are more open to new ideas, receptive to fresh influences, and ready to experiment with interesting new ingredients.

In *Savory to Sweet: Pies and Tarts*, Janice Murfitt provides new and unusual ways of adding flavor and interest to the basic pastries used, such as adding crushed nuts or citrus zest, and also presents a splendid array of fillings, both comfortingly traditional and classic with an intriguing twist. With these recipes she at long last gives tarts, savory and sweet, the recognition they deserve. As well as perfect treats to accompany tea and coffee, they make wonderful desserts, exciting first courses, satisfying and healthy light meals, and memorable party food.

Happy cooking!

ALBERT ROUX

INTRODUCTION

Sweet tarts are irresistible . . . jewel-bright fruit tarts decked with luscious berries and glazed with jam; or rich honeyed mixtures studded with nuts and dusted with confectioners' sugar to give a delicate appearance, yet hint at the delights hidden beneath . . . the temptation they present is overwhelming.

Savory tarts, often referred to as quiches, can also contain wonderful blends of herbs, vegetables, seafood, poultry, or meat, set in a rich creamy sauce to make satisfying first courses, light meals, or party snacks.

It is the pastry that contains these various fillings and sets them off by providing satisfying contrasts of textures. It can be formed and baked into many shapes and sizes and will offer different textures and flavors depending on the recipe.

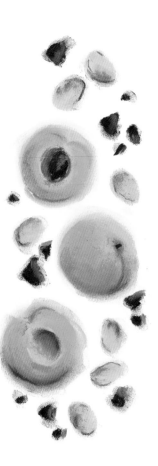

TYPES OF PASTRY

Basic pie pastry, which is the pastry most commonly used for savory tarts, is made with flour, shortening, and water and produces a crisp tart base. If the fats are changed (to, say, all butter or a mixture of half margarine and half shortening), it is quite noticeable how the pastry texture and flavor changes.

The addition of eggs, fruit juices, yogurt, or sour cream makes a richer pastry that, when baked, produces a crisp, light, and flaky result. When sugar is added to make a sweet pastry, the tart shells become almost like shortbread in texture and during baking color much more quickly.

Many flavoring ingredients can be introduced into the pastry, such as nuts, grated citrus zest, spices, chocolate, herbs, and seasonings. This not only adds variety to the taste and texture of the pastry shells but, teamed with the appropriate fillings, such flavored pastries can give an endless variety of wonderful flavor combinations.

MAKING PASTRY

Pastry is very simple to make, but unless care is taken when handling the dough, problems – such as uneven and shrunken pastry shells or hard dense textures – can arise. Most such pitfalls can be avoided by simply following a few easy guidelines when making the pastry:

★ Make sure all the ingredients are cold.

★ Measure all the ingredients carefully beforehand.

★ Sift the flour into a bowl first to add more air to the mixture and thus give lighter results.

★ Use fat that is cold and cut into pieces, so that when it is rubbed into the flour it breaks down evenly into fine "crumbs" and does not form a sticky, heavy mixture.

★ Add the measured amount of cold or chilled liquid gradually, mixing well with a fork until the dough begins to bind together. Too much liquid

makes a hard pastry that shrinks during cooking.

★ On a lightly floured surface, knead the dough lightly with the fingertips until it is smooth and free from cracks. Do not over-knead with hot hands. Use the dough immediately or wrap it in plastic wrap and keep it in a cool place until needed.

A food processor can be used to make the pastry, but take care not to over-work the mixture or it will form into a dough before the correct quantity of liquid has been added, which will produce pastry that is too short and very hard to handle.

ROLLING AND LINING

Roll out the pastry evenly on a lightly floured surface, keeping it in a neat shape that as far as possible matches the shape of the pan to be lined, whatever its size. Always roll only to and from you, never at angles or from side to side. Roll two or three times, then give the pastry a 90 degree turn and repeat the process. Keep doing this until the pastry is the right size and shape, or 1 inch larger all around than the pan to be lined.

Never stretch the pastry or it will shrink back during cooking to produce an uneven pastry shell.

To line a tart pan, drape the sheet of pastry over a rolling pin and ease it into the pan, molding it into the corners. Then press it gently up the side. Trim off the excess and press the sides of the pastry into any flutes on the sides of the pan.

When lining small tartlets and barquette molds, arrange them close together on a baking sheet and then lay the sheet of pastry loosely over the top. Using a little ball of pastry, ease the pastry sheet into each mold and then lightly run the rolling pin over the tops to cut off the excess. Finish the edges with a fork or your fingers.

Always prick the bottom of pastry shells all over with a fork to ensure that the pastry remains flat during baking. Chill at least 30 minutes to 1 hour – or even overnight – before baking to give the pastry time to rest. It will then retain its shape better during baking. However, do remember that a cold pastry shell will take longer to bake.

BAKING "BLIND" (UNFILLED)

It is usually a good idea to pre-bake a pastry shell before filling it, especially if it is to have a very liquid filling. Such baking "blind" ensures that the base is cooked and crisp and prevents the filling from soaking into the pastry to form a soggy layer at the bottom of the tart.

To bake a pastry shell "blind," first line it with wax paper and then half fill it with dried or ceramic baking beans. These both weigh it down and help conduct the heat evenly into the pastry during the cooking. Bake the prepared pastry shell 10–15 minutes, then remove the beans and paper and continue baking the pastry shell until the bottom is cooked and the edges are lightly browned, 5–10 minutes longer.

Sweet pastry shells will cook more quickly because of the sugar content. Egg in the dough will also help the pastry to keep its shape during baking and will give a nice golden color to the cooked shell.

TART PANS AND MOLDS

When one thinks of a tart, a round pastry usually springs to mind, but tarts can come in all manner of shapes and sizes depending on the pan or mold used. Apart from the traditional round ones, available in all sizes from very large to tiny tartlet molds, there are square, rectangular, and even decoratively shaped ones, such as those in the shape of a heart. All good kitchen supply stores have a wide range of such tart pans.

Round loose-bottomed tart pans with plain or fluted edges are the most popular as they are so easy to line with pastry. When baked, the loose bottom allows for easier removal of the tart from the mold.

The most popular tart pan in France is the "tranche" (meaning "slice"). Elongated rectangles in shape, these come either as loose-bottomed fluted pans or as straight-sided forms that must be placed on a baking sheet. The long, narrow tarts produced by these pans need careful handling when they are being unmolded and cut.

Individual tartlet or barquette molds are made in sizes that vary from the very tiny (1 inch across) up to diameters of about 6 inches and are mainly used for party or special occasion food. The larger molds come with loose bottoms for easier use. Ensure that rigid pans are well greased before use.

USING READY-MADE PASTRY

In this fast-moving world we often simply don't have the time to spend doing much preparation in the kitchen, so it is always helpful to use convenient shortcuts. As appropriate, ready-made frozen pie and puff pastries and packaged pastry mixes will work well in place of the pastries I have suggested.

As you will see, however, the pastry recipes I have given have been carefully devised to complement the filling used. Flavoring ingredients such as herbs and spices, cheeses, and seasonings have been added to the savory tarts, tartlets, and barquettes to give even more mouthwatering results. Likewise the pastry shells for the sweet tarts have been enlivened with added sugar, citrus zest, nuts, or chocolate to enhance their flavor.

If you want to take advantage of store-bought pastries it is possible to add the extra flavoring ingredients to a packaged pastry mix. Ready-made pastry, however, is not quite so receptive to the addition of ingredients. It is inadvisable to add sugar to it, for instance, but confectioners' sugar can be used to dust the work surface instead of flour prior to rolling. Nuts, citrus zest, herbs, and spices can also be lightly kneaded into ready-made pastry, but care must be taken not to over-knead, or the pastry will become hard and unworkable.

TARTLETS AND BARQUETTES

*I*ndividually fashioned pastry tartlets are always appealing and evocative of nursery rhymes and childhood treats, but they also have the added advantage of being easier to serve and store. Savory versions make wonderful snacks, light lunches, or first courses, and a selection of them could also be served to accompany cocktails or as part of a buffet meal or picnic. Sweet tartlets are also excellent for lunch boxes and al fresco eating, as well as for serving with coffee and afternoon tea.

The French term "barquettes" refers to boat-shaped tartlets, which are popular in haute cuisine as hors d'oeuvres. Their shape makes a pleasing change and suits them particularly well to large attractive displays.

Clockwise from the top: Camembert and Cranberry Barquettes (page 12); Gruyère and Prosciutto Barquettes (page 13); a Goat Cheese and Herb Tartlet (page 12)

When buying
Camembert cheese
for the
CAMEMBERT AND
CRANBERRY
BARQUETTES, *try
to buy a slightly
under-ripe cheese as
this will slice more
easily.*

For the GOAT
CHEESE AND HERB
TARTLETS, *buy a
goat cheese that has
no flavored coating
and is quite soft in
texture.*

PROSCIUTTO *is a
traditional Italian
ham. The pigs are
fed on a diet of
whey left over from
making the local
Parmesan cheese
and the ham is dry-
cured under weights
and left to mature
for one year. It is
very thinly sliced
and served raw as
an appetizer or used
as a flavoring in
cooking.*

CAMEMBERT AND CRANBERRY BARQUETTES

MAKES 16

FOR THE PASTRY
¾ cup flour
½ tsp salt
½ tsp English mustard powder
6 tbsp butter, cut into small pieces
1 egg yolk
FOR THE FILLING
2 tbsp orange juice
1 tbsp sugar
½ cup fresh or frozen cranberries
¼ lb Camembert cheese, thinly sliced

To make the pastry: Sift the flour, salt, and mustard powder into a bowl, add the butter, and rub it in finely with your fingertips. Stir in the egg yolk and mix together with a fork to form a firm dough.

Knead the dough on a lightly floured surface until smooth. Roll it out thinly and use to line sixteen 4-inch fluted barquette molds. Chill 30 minutes.

Preheat the oven to 400°F.

Bake the pastry shells "blind" until lightly browned at the edges and cooked, about 10 minutes.

While they are baking make the filling: Place the orange juice, sugar, and cranberries in a small saucepan. Heat gently, shaking the pan occasionally, until the cranberries are tender and the liquid has evaporated. Let the cranberries cool.

Arrange a little cheese in each pastry shell. Just before serving, place the pastry boats in the oven until the cheese has melted, 2–3 minutes. Remove them from the oven and arrange a few cranberries in each barquette. Serve immediately.

GOAT CHEESE AND HERB TARTLETS★

MAKES 4

FOR THE PASTRY
¾ cup flour
½ tsp salt and ¼ tsp freshly ground black pepper
6 tbsp butter, cut into small pieces
1 egg yolk
FOR THE FILLING
¼ lb soft goat cheese
2 tbsp chopped mixed fresh herbs, including basil,
marjoram, and parsley
2 tbsp minced scallion
1 egg
(★see page 2 for advice on eggs)
⅔ cup light cream
½ tsp freshly ground black pepper

To make the pastry: Sift the flour, salt, and pepper into a bowl. Add the butter and rub it in finely with your fingertips. Stir in the egg yolk and mix together with a fork to form a firm dough.

Knead the dough on a lightly floured surface until smooth. Roll it out thinly and use to line four 4½-inch round loose-bottomed fluted tartlet molds. Chill 30 minutes.

Preheat the oven to 400°F.

Bake the shells "blind" until lightly browned at the edges and cooked on the bottom, about 10 minutes. Reduce the oven temperature to 375°F.

While they are baking make the filling: Place the cheese, herbs, and scallion in a bowl and beat together until well blended. Add the egg, cream, and pepper and beat again until well blended.

Pour the filling into the pastry shells and return them to the cooler oven to bake until the filling has just set, 10–15 minutes longer. Serve warm or cold.

GRUYÈRE AND PROSCIUTTO BARQUETTES★

MAKES 6

FOR THE PASTRY
¾ cup flour
½ tsp salt and ¼ tsp freshly ground pepper
6 tbsp butter, cut into small pieces
1 egg yolk
1 tbsp chopped fresh basil
FOR THE FILLING
3 oz Gruyère cheese, thinly sliced
2 oz prosciutto, cut into strips
⅔ cup light cream
1 egg
(★see page 2 for advice on eggs)
½ tsp Dijon-style mustard
¼ tsp freshly ground pepper

To make the pastry: Sift the flour, salt, and pepper into a bowl, add the butter, and rub it in finely with your fingertips. Stir in the egg yolk and basil and mix together with a fork to form a firm dough.

Knead the dough on a lightly floured surface until smooth. Roll it out thinly and use to line six 6-inch barquette molds. Chill 30 minutes.

Preheat the oven to 400°F.

Bake the shells "blind" until lightly browned at the edges and cooked on the bottom, about 10 minutes. Reduce the oven temperature to 375°F.

While they are baking make the filling. Arrange the cheese slices in the pastry shells with the strips of prosciutto on top. In a bowl, whisk together the cream, egg, mustard, and pepper.

Spoon the egg mixture into the pastry shells and return them to the cooler oven to bake until the filling has just set, about 15 minutes. Serve warm or cold.

QUAIL EGGS, *from farmed quail, can be ordered from specialty markets. They are difficult to peel when cooked, so allow plenty of time.*

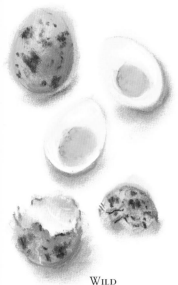

WILD MUSHROOMS, *such as chanterelles and cèpes, have deep interesting flavors and are now available in specialty markets and better supermarkets.*

BARQUETTES OF QUAIL EGGS WITH CHERVIL

MAKES 20

FOR THE PASTRY
*¾ cup flour
6 tbsp butter, cut into small pieces
1 tbsp freshly grated Parmesan cheese
1 egg*
FOR THE FILLING
*2 egg yolks
1 tbsp raspberry vinegar
¼ tsp each salt and freshly ground black pepper
6 tbsp unsalted butter
½ tsp Dijon-style mustard
2 tbsp chopped fresh chervil or parsley
20 quail eggs, hard-cooked, peeled and halved
½ tsp ground mace*

Make the pastry: Sift the flour into a bowl, add the butter, and rub in finely with your fingertips. Stir in the Parmesan and egg and mix to a firm dough.

Knead the dough on a lightly floured surface until smooth. Roll out thinly and use to line twenty 3½-inch barquette molds. Chill 30 minutes.

Preheat the oven to 400°F.

Bake the barquette shells "blind" until lightly browned at the edges, about 10 minutes.

While they are baking make the filling: Whisk together the egg yolks, vinegar, salt, and pepper.

Melt the butter over a low heat until foaming. Very gradually add this to the filling mixture while still whisking until all has been added and the filling is creamy and thick. Stir in the mustard and chervil.

Arrange the two halves of each quail egg in each pastry boat and carefully spoon the sauce over to cover evenly. Sprinkle lightly with the mace.

Return the pastry boats to the oven to bake until the sauce bubbles, 2–3 minutes. Alternatively, broil them 1–2 minutes. Serve immediately.

WILD MUSHROOM AND OREGANO BARQUETTES

MAKES 8

FOR THE PASTRY
*¾ cup flour
½ tsp salt and ¼ tsp freshly ground black pepper
6 tbsp butter, cut into small pieces
1 egg yolk*
FOR THE FILLING
*2 tbsp butter
2 tbsp chopped fresh oregano
3 oz fresh wild or oyster mushrooms
1 tbsp flour
1 tsp finely grated zest and 2 tsp juice from a washed lime
1 tbsp Marsala wine
¼ cup whipping cream
2 tbsp chopped fresh chives
½ tsp salt and ¼ tsp freshly ground black pepper*

Make the pastry: Sift flour, salt, and pepper into a bowl, rub in the butter finely with your fingertips. Stir in the egg yolk and mix to a firm dough.

Knead the dough on a lightly floured surface until smooth. Roll it out thinly and use to line eight 4-inch barquette molds. Chill 30 minutes.

Preheat the oven to 400°F. Bake shells "blind" until lightly browned at the edges, about 10 minutes.

Melt the butter in a saucepan over medium heat, stir in the oregano and mushrooms, and cook 1–2 minutes. Add the flour, stir until well blended, and cook 30 seconds. Then add the lime zest and juice and the Marsala and bring to a boil, stirring. Cook 1 minute longer, stirring constantly.

Off the heat, stir in the cream, chives, salt, and pepper. Spoon into the shells. Serve warm or cold.

Top: Wild Mushroom and Oregano Barquettes; bottom: Barquettes of Quail Eggs with Chervil

SHRIMP AND FENNEL TARTLETS★

MAKES 6

FOR THE PASTRY
¾ cup flour
½ tsp salt and ¼ tsp freshly ground black pepper
6 tbsp butter, cut into small pieces
1 egg yolk
FOR THE FILLING
2 tbsp butter
⅓ chopped bulb fennel, including some of the frond
1 garlic clove, minced
6 tbsp mayonnaise
2 tbsp whipping cream
1 egg
(★see page 2 for advice on eggs)
¼ tsp salt and ¼ tsp freshly ground black pepper
6 large cooked shrimp, peeled, deveined, and sliced

Make the pastry: Sift flour, salt, and pepper into a bowl. Rub in the butter finely with your fingertips. Stir in the egg yolk and mix to a firm dough.

Knead the dough on a lightly floured surface until smooth. Roll it out thinly and use to line six 3½-inch tartlet molds. Chill 30 minutes.

Preheat the oven to 400°F.

Bake the pastry shells "blind" until lightly browned at the edges, about 10 minutes. Reduce the oven temperature to 375°F.

While they are baking make the filling: Melt the butter in a heavy saucepan over medium heat, stir in the fennel and garlic, and cook quickly for 1 minute. Remove the pan from the heat.

In a bowl, beat together the mayonnaise, cream, egg, salt, and pepper. Stir in the fennel mixture.

Divide the shrimp among the pastry shells and spoon over the fennel mixture. Return the tartlets to the oven and bake until the filling has just set, about 15 minutes. Serve warm or cold.

SORREL AND PIKE TARTLETS★

MAKES 6

FOR THE PASTRY
¾ cup flour
½ tsp salt and ¼ tsp freshly ground black pepper
6 tbsp butter, cut into small pieces
1 egg yolk
FOR THE FILLING
2 tbsp butter
2 tbsp minced scallion
½ cup chopped sorrel leaves
6 oz fillets of pike or any other meaty white fish, cut into small pieces
¼ tsp salt and ¼ tsp freshly ground black pepper
1 egg
(★see page 2 for advice on eggs)
⅔ cup light cream
1 tsp ground mace

To make the pastry: Sift the flour, salt, and pepper into a bowl, add the butter, and rub it in finely with your fingertips. Stir in the egg yolk and mix together with a fork to form a firm dough.

Knead the dough on a lightly floured surface until smooth. Roll it out thinly and use to line six 3-inch round tartlet molds. Chill 30 minutes.

Preheat the oven to 400°F.

Bake the pastry shells "blind" until lightly browned at the edges, about 10 minutes. Reduce the oven temperature to 375°F.

While they are baking make the filling: Melt the butter in a saucepan over medium heat and add the scallion and sorrel. Cook quickly for 1 minute, stirring. Stir in the pike, salt, and pepper.

Beat the egg, cream, and mace together, stir in the fish mixture, and spoon into the tartlet shells.

Return tartlets to the oven to bake until filling has just set, 15–20 minutes. Serve warm or cold.

PORT AND FIG BARQUETTES

MAKES 8

FOR THE PASTRY
¾ cup flour
6 tbsp butter, cut into small pieces
2 tbsp sugar
1 egg yolk
FOR THE FILLING
½ cup ruby port wine
1 tsp finely grated zest and 2 tbsp juice from a washed orange
2 whole cloves
7 tbsp sugar
4 fresh, firm figs
2 tsp arrowroot
⅔ cup whipping cream, whipped to soft peaks

Make the pastry: Sift the flour into a bowl, add the butter, and rub in finely with your fingertips. Stir in the sugar and egg yolk and mix to a firm dough.

Knead the dough on a lightly floured surface until smooth. Roll it out thinly and use to line eight 4-inch barquette molds. Chill 30 minutes.

Preheat the oven to 400°F.

Bake the pastry shells "blind" until lightly browned at the edges, about 10 minutes. Let cool.

Make the filling: Place the port, orange zest and juice, cloves, and sugar in a saucepan. Heat gently, stirring occasionally, until the sugar has dissolved.

Add the figs, cover, and cook over low heat gently until the figs are tender, 4–5 minutes. Using a slotted spoon, transfer the figs to a plate and let cool.

Blend the arrowroot with 1 tablespoon of cold water and add to the port syrup. Bring to a boil, stirring constantly until thickened, and simmer 1 minute. Strain.

Spoon the cream into the pastry shells. Cut each fig into 6 wedges and arrange 3 in each pastry shell. Spoon the syrup glaze over the fruit and let set.

Sorrel is a soft-leaf green herb that is similar to baby spinach in appearance. It has a rich, sharp flavor and goes well with salmon. It can be made into a sauce or used to flavor soups and omelettes. Look for fresh, firm leaves. Do not keep them more than 2–3 days, stored in a plastic bag in the refrigerator.

BLACKBERRY AND TANSY TARTLETS★

MAKES 6

FOR THE PASTRY
¾ cup flour
6 tbsp butter, cut into small pieces
2 tbsp sugar
1 egg yolk
FOR THE FILLING
1 egg
(★see page 2 for advice on eggs)
6 tbsp sugar
⅔ cup whipping cream
3 tansy or lemon balm leaves
1 pint blackberries
2 tsp arrowroot

TANSY *is an ancient English herb used mainly for its medicinal and tonic qualities. It was traditionally used to flavor cakes and custards, in sparing quantities because of its bitter flavor. Its leaves are soft and feathery and in summer it bears bright yellow button flowers.*

To make the pastry: Sift the flour into a bowl, add the butter, and rub it in finely with your fingertips. Stir in the sugar and egg yolk and mix together with a fork to form a firm dough.

Knead the dough on a lightly floured surface until smooth. Roll it out thinly and use to line six 3½-inch heart-shaped tartlet molds. Chill 30 minutes. Preheat the oven to 400°F.

Bake the shells "blind" until lightly browned at the edges and cooked on the bottom, about 10 minutes. Reduce the oven temperature to 325°F.

While they are baking make the filling: Place the egg, 2 tablespoons sugar, and the cream in a bowl and whisk until well blended. Half fill the pastry shells with the custard and place half a tansy or lemon balm leaf in each. Return the tartlets to the oven to bake until the custard has just set, about 20 minutes. Let cool and then remove the pieces of leaf.

While they are cooling place the blackberries and remaining sugar in a saucepan with 2 tablespoons of water. Heat gently, shaking the pan occasionally, until the blackberries are tender but still whole.

Drain the blackberries and reserve the juice, adding water, if necessary to make ⅔ cup. Blend the arrowroot with 1 tablespoon of cold water and stir it into the blackberry juice.

Return the juice to the saucepan, bring to a boil, stirring, and simmer 1 minute. Fill each tartlet with blackberries and spoon the blackberry glaze over the fruit to cover evenly. Let set.

BLOSSOM PINK TARTLETS★

MAKES 12

FOR THE PASTRY
1⅓ cups flour
10 tbsp butter, cut into small pieces
2 tbsp sugar
1 egg, beaten
FOR THE FILLING
⅔ cup unsweetened apple juice
1 tbsp sugar
¾ lb apples, peeled, cored, and thinly sliced
1 small banana, mashed
2 tsp unflavored gelatin
¼ cup sweetened condensed milk
2 tsp finely grated zest and 2 tbsp juice
from a washed lemon
1 egg, separated
(★see page 2 for advice on eggs)
pink food coloring

Make the pastry: Sift the flour into a bowl, add the butter, and rub in finely with your fingertips. Stir in the sugar and egg and mix together to form a firm dough.

Knead the dough on a lightly floured surface until smooth. Roll it out thinly and use to line twelve 3-inch diameter brioche molds. Chill 30 minutes.

Preheat the oven to 400°F.

Bake the tartlet shells "blind" until lightly browned at the edges and cooked on the bottom, 10–15 minutes. Let cool.

While they are baking and cooling make the filling: Place the apple juice and sugar in a heavy saucepan, bring to a boil, and add the sliced apples. Cover and cook gently over low heat until the apple slices are tender, 2–3 minutes. Using a slotted spoon, remove the apples and place them in a bowl with the banana. Mix together well and let cool.

Sprinkle the gelatin into the apple syrup and stir until dissolved. Let cool. Beat together the condensed milk, lemon zest, juice, and egg yolk until smooth and spoon into the pastry shells. Let set.

Place the egg white, apple syrup, and a few drops of pink food coloring in a bowl and beat constantly until thick and foamy.

Spoon the fruit onto the custard in the shells and top with the apple foam. Let set in the refrigerator.

MARSALA CREAM BARQUETTES

MAKES 8

FOR THE PASTRY
¾ cup flour
6 tbsp butter, cut into small pieces
2 tbsp sugar
1 egg yolk
FOR THE FILLING
3 egg yolks
5 tbsp flour
2 tbsp sugar
3 tbsp Marsala wine
⅔ cup milk
¾ cup whipping cream
3 oz semisweet chocolate, melted
FOR DECORATION
white and dark chocolate curls

To make the pastry: Sift the flour into a bowl, add the butter, and rub it in finely with your fingertips. Stir in the sugar and egg yolk and mix together with a fork to form a firm dough.

Knead the dough on a lightly floured surface until smooth. Roll it out thinly and use to line eight 4-inch barquette molds. Chill 30 minutes.

Preheat the oven to 400°F.

Bake the pastry shells "blind" until lightly browned at the edges and cooked on the bottom, about 10 minutes.

While they are baking make the filling: Place the egg yolks, flour, sugar, and Marsala in a bowl and whisk together until well blended. Bring the milk to a boil in a small pan and pour it over the egg mixture, whisking constantly.

Return the custard to the saucepan and cook over low heat, stirring constantly, until the custard thickens. Cook 1 minute, then remove the pan from the heat. Stir in the cream. Let cool.

Brush the inside of each pastry shell with melted chocolate to coat evenly. Chill until set.

Put the cream mixture in a pastry bag fitted with a medium star tip. Pipe the filling into each pastry shell.

Decorate with chocolate curls before serving.

MARSALA *is a fortified dessert wine from Sicily. A proportion of brandy is added to the local wine and part of this is heated to give the characteristic caramel flavor. It is used extensively in dessert recipes and is the essential flavoring for the Italian custard dessert Zabaglione.*

CHOCOLATE CURLS *are made by shaving a bar of chocolate, at room temperature, with a vegetable peeler.*

MAIDS OF HONOR, it is said, were the favorite cakes of Ann Boleyn, the second wife of Henry VIII, but other stories suggest the recipe originated during the reign of her daughter, Queen Elizabeth I.

RENNET is an enzyme found in the lining of a calf's stomach. When added to lukewarm milk, it thickens the milk and separates it into solid curds and whey, the milky-white liquid. It is made commercially and sold in most specialty markets and supermarkets.

MAIDS OF HONOR

MAKES 12

½ lb frozen puff pastry, thawed
FOR THE FILLING
2½ cups milk
2 tbsp sugar
1 lemon balm leaf
1 tsp powdered rennet
2 tbsp butter, melted
1 egg, beaten
⅓ cup ground almonds
½ tsp finely grated zest from a washed lemon
½ tsp grated nutmeg
1 tbsp dried currants
FOR DECORATION
confectioners' sugar

On a lightly floured surface, roll out the pastry to a thickness of about ⅛ inch. Using a cutter that is ½ inch greater in diameter than the tops of the tartlet molds being used, cut out 12 pastry rounds and use to line 12 tartlet molds. Chill until required.

Make the filling: Place the milk, sugar, and lemon leaf in a pan and heat gently until lukewarm. Off the heat, stir in the rennet, and leave in a warm place until thick, about 5 minutes.

Place a cheesecloth-lined strainer over a bowl. Pour in the milk mixture and let it drain and separate at least 4 hours. Remove and discard the lemon balm leaf. Preheat the oven to 425°F.

Place the curds, butter, egg, ground almonds, lemon zest, and nutmeg in a bowl. Mix together until well blended. Spoon the mixture into the pastry shells and sprinkle each with a few currants.

Bake until risen and lightly browned, about 20 minutes. Let cool in the molds 5 minutes, then remove carefully and cool on a wire rack. The filling will sink slightly.

When cold, dust with confectioners' sugar.

SUMMER FRUIT TARTLETS

MAKES 18

FOR THE PASTRY
¾ cup flour
6 tbsp butter, cut into small pieces
2 tbsp sugar
1 egg yolk
FOR THE FILLING
¾ cup whipping cream
1 tbsp rose water
1 tbsp confectioners' sugar
½ cup apricot jam, boiled and strained
¾ lb mixed fruits, such as raspberries, red currants, black currants and white currants, wild strawberries, seedless grapes, blueberries, and sliced pitted nectarines

To make the pastry: Sift the flour into a bowl, add the butter, and rub it in finely with your fingertips. Stir in the sugar and egg yolk and mix together with a fork to form a firm dough. Knead the dough on a lightly floured surface until smooth. Roll it out thinly and use to line eighteen 3-inch round fluted tartlet molds. Chill 30 minutes.

Preheat the oven to 400°F.

Bake the pastry shells "blind" until lightly browned at the edges and cooked on the bottom, about 10 minutes. Let cool.

While they are baking and cooling make the filling: Place the cream, rose water, and sugar in a bowl and beat until just thick. Put in a pastry bag fitted with a small plain tip.

Brush the inside of each shell with some of the apricot jam and pipe a little of the cream mixture into each. Arrange the fruits on top and brush with more of the apricot glaze. Let set.

Top left: a heart-shaped Blackberry and Tansy Tartlet (page 18); rest of page: assorted Summer Fruit Tartlets

SAVORY TARTS

About twenty years ago, the sudden vogue in this country for the French quiche marked a revival of the old-fashioned tradition of making tarts with savory fillings. Since then all manner of imaginative variations on the theme and new inspired combinations have found their way into our repertoires. Savory tarts work well as snacks and as lunches or light meals, with an accompanying salad. They also make useful first courses and memorable party food. Usually with a rich custard base, fillings can be as varied as the range of fresh ingredients available. Using fresh herbs and spices and exploiting the wide range of different tasty cheeses can also make interesting dishes for vegetarians.

Top: Salmon and Sorrel Tart (page 25); bottom: Asparagus and Dill Tart (page 28)

CRAB TART WITH CREAM AND BASIL

SERVES 4–6

6 sheets of phyllo pastry
4 tbsp butter, melted
FOR THE FILLING
2 tbsp butter
½ cup minced fresh chives
2 tbsp minced fresh basil
2 tbsp minced fresh chervil or parsley
6 oz fresh crab meat
⅔ cup sour cream
2 eggs
½ tsp salt
¼ tsp cayenne pepper
¼ tsp hot pepper sauce

Preheat the oven to 400°F. Brush the sheets of phyllo pastry generously with melted butter and arrange them in layers to cover the bottom and sides of an 8-inch long shallow oval baking dish. Tuck the overhanging excess pastry in to make a neat edge.

To make the filling: Melt the butter in a saucepan, add the chives, basil, and chervil, and cook quickly for 1 minute, stirring constantly.

Remove the saucepan from the heat and stir in the crab meat.

In a bowl, beat together the sour cream, eggs, salt, cayenne, and hot pepper sauce. Add this to the crab mixture and stir until well blended.

Pour the crab mixture into a pastry-lined dish, sprinkle with cayenne, and bake until the pastry is golden brown and the filling has just set, 20–25 minutes.

Serve warm or cold.

Top: Crab Tart with Cream and Basil; bottom: Mussel Tart

MUSSEL TART

SERVES 6

FOR THE PASTRY
1¼ cups flour
½ tsp salt
1 stick butter, cut into small pieces
1 tbsp lemon juice

FOR THE FILLING
2 tbsp butter
1 tbsp oil
1 onion, thinly sliced
1 garlic clove, minced
3 oz oyster mushrooms, sliced
3 fresh bay leaves
2 tsp each chopped fresh rosemary, thyme, and parsley
12 cherry tomatoes, halved
¼ cup white wine
⅔ cup light cream
2 eggs
½ tsp salt and ¼ tsp freshly ground black pepper
10 shucked fresh mussels, halved

Make the pastry: Sift flour and salt into a bowl, rub the butter in finely. Stir in the lemon juice and 2–3 tablespoons of cold water. Mix to a firm dough.

Knead until smooth. Roll thinly and use to line a 9-inch round tart or pie pan. Flute the edges. Chill briefly. Preheat the oven to 400°F.

Bake the pastry shell "blind" until lightly browned at the edges, 10–15 minutes.

Melt the butter with the oil in a pan over medium-high heat. Add the onion and garlic and cook quickly 1 minute. Add the mushrooms, herbs, and tomatoes and stir 1 minute longer. Add the wine, bring to a boil, and remove from the heat.

Beat together the cream, eggs, salt, and pepper and add to the pan with the mussels. Mix well.

Pour into the shell and bake until set and lightly browned, 15–20 minutes. Serve warm or cold.

SALMON AND SORREL TART★

SERVES 6

FOR THE PASTRY
1¼ cups flour
½ tsp salt and ¼ tsp freshly ground black pepper
1 stick butter, cut into small pieces
1 tbsp lemon juice

FOR THE FILLING
½ lb skinless salmon fillet, cut into small pieces
1 tbsp raspberry vinegar
1 tbsp pink peppercorns
2 oz sorrel leaves
½ cup ricotta or cream cheese
⅔ cup light cream
2 egg yolks
(★see page 2 for advice on eggs)
¼ tsp salt

To make the pastry: Sift the flour, salt, and pepper into a bowl, add the butter, and rub it in finely with your fingertips. Stir in the lemon juice and 1–2 tablespoons of cold water and mix to a firm dough.

Knead until smooth. Roll thinly and use to line an 8-inch square loose-bottomed tart pan. Chill 30 minutes. Preheat the oven to 400°F.

Bake the pastry shell "blind" until lightly browned at the edges, 10–15 minutes. Remove from the oven and reduce the temperature to 350°F.

While the shell is baking make the filling: Place the salmon in a bowl with the raspberry vinegar and peppercorns and let marinate.

Blanch the sorrel in boiling water 1 minute. Drain and chop finely. Beat together with the cheese. Spread the cheese mixture over the bottom of the pastry shell and top with the salmon mixture.

Beat together the cream, egg yolks, and salt and pour over the salmon mixture. Bake the tart until the filling has just set, 25–30 minutes. Cool in the pan, then remove. Serve warm or cold.

PHYLLO, *from the Greek word for "leaf," is comprised of sheets of wafer-thin pastry. It can be used for both sweet and savory dishes and when baked or fried has a light, crisp texture. Care must be taken not to allow phyllo to dry out as it then breaks readily, so keep it covered with a damp towel and remove the sheets one at a time.*

PINK PEPPERCORNS *are not really peppercorns at all, but a processed berry imported from Madagascar.*

GARAM MASALA, *meaning "hot spice mixture," is an intensely aromatic blend of ground spices used in some Indian recipes. It is available commercially, but it is possible to grind your own garam masala. There are many different blends, but most use coriander, cumin, cardamom, ginger, cloves, and black pepper.*

The famous French tart, QUICHE LORRAINE, was first made in the province of Alsace-Lorraine. Traditionally it was made with strips of fat salt pork or unsmoked bacon set in a well-flavored cheese custard.

SPICED CHICKEN TART★

SERVES 6

6 oz frozen puff pastry, thawed
FOR THE FILLING
2 tbsp butter or margarine
1 leek, thinly sliced
1 garlic clove, minced
½ tsp ground turmeric
2 tsp ground cumin
2 tsp garam masala
½ lb chicken breast meat, diced
1 potato, peeled, diced, and cooked
1 tbsp chopped fresh coriander (cilantro)
grated zest and juice of 1 washed lime
½ tsp salt and ¼ tsp freshly ground black pepper
1 tbsp mango chutney
⅔ cup light cream
2 eggs
(★see page 2 for advice on eggs)
FOR GARNISH
sprigs of fresh coriander (cilantro)

Roll out the pastry thinly on a lightly floured surface and use it to line a 9-inch round tart or pie pan. Flute the edges and chill 30 minutes.

Preheat the oven to 400°F.

Bake the pastry shell "blind" until lightly browned at the edges, 10–15 minutes.

While the shell is baking make the filling: Melt the butter or margarine in a saucepan over medium heat. Add the leek and garlic and cook quickly for 1 minute. Stir in the spices, chicken, and potato. Cook, stirring frequently, until the chicken has turned white. Add the coriander, lime zest, juice, salt, pepper, and chutney. Remove from the heat.

Beat together the cream and eggs and stir into the chicken mixture. Pour into the pastry shell and bake until the filling has set, 15–20 minutes.

Serve hot or cold, garnished with coriander.

QUICHE LORRAINE★

SERVES 6

FOR THE PASTRY
1¼ cups flour
½ tsp salt
1 stick butter, cut into small pieces
1 tbsp lemon juice
FOR THE FILLING
¼ lb unsmoked bacon, fried and crumbled
1½ cups grated Gruyère cheese
4 egg yolks
(★see page 2 for advice on eggs)
1¼ cups light cream
1 tsp freshly grated nutmeg
¼ tsp freshly ground black pepper
1 tsp Dijon-style mustard

Make the pastry: Sift the flour and salt into a bowl, add the butter, and rub it in finely with your fingertips. Stir in the lemon juice and 2 tablespoons of cold water and mix to a firm dough.

Knead the dough on a lightly floured surface until smooth. Roll it out thinly and use to line a 9-inch round loose-bottomed fluted tart pan. Chill 30 minutes.

Preheat the oven to 400°F.

Bake the pastry shell "blind" until lightly browned at the edges, 10–15 minutes. Reduce the oven temperature to 350°F.

Scatter the bacon and cheese over the bottom of the pastry shell.

In a bowl, beat together the egg yolks, cream, nutmeg, pepper, and mustard until well blended.

Pour into the shell, return it to the oven, and bake until the filling has just set, 25–30 minutes. Cool in the pan, then remove and serve warm or cold.

Top: Spiced Chicken Tart; bottom: Chicken Liver and Red Currant Tart (page 28)

CHICKEN LIVER AND RED CURRANT TART★

SERVES 4–6

FOR THE PASTRY
¾ cup whole wheat flour
½ cup + 2 tbsp all-purpose flour, sifted
6 tbsp butter or margarine, cut into small pieces
1 tsp chopped fresh rosemary
FOR THE FILLING
2 tbsp butter
3 scallions, thinly sliced
1 garlic clove, minced
2 tsp chopped fresh rosemary
6 oz chicken livers, chopped
2 tbsp Marsala wine
¼ cup sour cream
1 egg
(★see page 2 for advice on eggs)
½ tsp salt and ¼ tsp freshly ground black pepper
½ cup red currants
FOR GARNISH
sprigs of fresh rosemary

To make the pastry: Sift the flours into a bowl, add the butter or margarine, and rub it in finely with your fingertips. Stir in the rosemary and 3–4 tablespoons of cold water and mix to a firm dough.

Knead on a lightly floured surface until smooth. Roll it out thinly and use to line a 14-×4-inch rectangular loose-bottomed tart pan or form set on a baking sheet. Chill 30 minutes.

Preheat the oven to 400°F.

Bake the pastry shell "blind" until lightly browned at the edges, 10–15 minutes.

While it is baking make the filling: Melt the butter in a frying pan over medium-high heat, add the scallions, garlic, and rosemary, and cook for 1 minute. Add the livers and fry until browned 1–2 minutes. Stir in Marsala and remove from heat.

In a bowl, beat together the sour cream, egg, salt, and pepper. Add this to the liver mixture and stir gently until well blended. Reserving a whole stem of red currants, remove the remaining stems and add the red currants to the liver mixture.

Pour the mixture into the pastry shell and level the top. Return it to the oven and bake until the filling has just set, 15–20 minutes.

Let cool in the pan 5 minutes, then remove carefully. Serve hot or cold, garnished with sprigs of rosemary and the reserved red currants.

ASPARAGUS AND DILL TART★

SERVES 6

FOR THE PASTRY
1¼ cups flour
½ tsp salt and ¼ tsp freshly ground black pepper
¼ tsp English mustard powder
6 tbsp butter or margarine, cut into small pieces
½ cup finely grated Cheddar cheese
1 egg yolk
FOR THE FILLING
6 oz asparagus tips
1 egg + 1 extra yolk
(★see page 2 for advice on eggs)
1¼ cups light cream
½ tsp salt and ¼ tsp finely ground black pepper
3 tbsp chopped fresh dill
2 tsp Dijon-style mustard

To make the pastry: Sift the flour, salt, pepper, and mustard powder into a bowl, add the butter or margarine, and rub it in finely with your fingertips. Stir in the cheese, egg yolk, and 1–2 tablespoons of cold water and mix together to a firm dough.

Knead the dough on a lightly floured surface until smooth. Roll it out thinly and use to line a

14-×4-inch rectangular loose-bottomed tart pan or form set on a baking sheet. Chill 30 minutes.

Preheat the oven to 400°F.

Bake the pastry shell "blind" until lightly browned at the edges and cooked on the bottom, 10–15 minutes. Reduce the oven temperature to 350°F.

While the shell is baking make the filling: Cook the asparagus in boiling water 1 minute, then drain well. In a bowl beat together the egg and egg yolk, cream, salt, pepper, dill, and mustard until well blended. Pour this filling into the pastry shell and arrange the asparagus tips on top.

Return to the cooler oven and bake until the filling has just set, 20–25 minutes. Let cool in the pan, then remove carefully and serve warm or cold.

SPINACH AND RAISIN TART★

SERVES 4–6

FOR THE PASTRY
¾ cup flour
½ tsp salt
4 tbsp butter or margarine, cut into small pieces
1 tbsp lemon juice
FOR THE FILLING
½ lb fresh spinach leaves
2 eggs
(★see page 2 for advice on eggs)
¾ cup thick plain yogurt
½ tsp salt and ¼ tsp finely ground black pepper
1 tsp freshly grated nutmeg
⅓ cup raisins

To make the pastry: Sift the flour and salt into a bowl, add the butter or margarine, and rub it in finely with your fingertips. Stir in the lemon juice and 2–3 tablespoons of cold water and mix together with a fork to form a firm dough.

Knead on a lightly floured surface until smooth. Roll it out thinly and use to line an 8-inch round loose-bottomed fluted tart pan. Chill 30 minutes.

Preheat the oven to 400°F.

Bake the pastry shell "blind" until lightly browned at the edges and cooked on the bottom, 10–15 minutes. Remove from the oven, and reduce the oven temperature to 350°F.

While the shell is baking, make the filling: Blanch the spinach in boiling water for 1 minute. Drain well and chop finely.

Place the eggs, yogurt, salt, pepper, and nutmeg in a bowl and beat them together until well blended. Stir in the spinach and raisins and pour the mixture into the pastry shell. Return the tart to the cooler oven and bake until the filling has set, 20–25 minutes.

Let cool in the pan, then remove it carefully. Serve warm or cold.

ASPARAGUS *is in season from February through June. When buying asparagus, look for tightly closed "buds" or tips and fresh green, unwrinkled stalks. Nowadays, ready-trimmed tips are available from supermarkets, but you can use the stalks for soups and sauces.*

FRESH HERB AND GARLIC TART⋆

SERVES 4

FOR THE PASTRY
¾ cup flour
1 tbsp freshly grated Parmesan cheese
¼ tsp English mustard powder
½ tsp salt and ¼ tsp freshly ground black pepper
4 tbsp butter or margarine, cut into small pieces

FOR THE FILLING
2 garlic cloves, minced
¼ cup chopped mixed fresh herbs, including parsley,
rosemary, oregano, and basil
½ cup ricotta or cream cheese
¼ cup thick plain yogurt
2 eggs, beaten
(⋆see page 2 for advice on eggs)
½ tsp salt and ¼ tsp freshly ground black pepper

To make the pastry: Sift the flour, Parmesan, mustard, salt, and pepper into a bowl. Add the butter or margarine and rub it in finely with your fingertips. Stir in 2–3 tablespoons of cold water and mix together with a fork to form a firm dough.

Knead on a lightly floured surface until smooth. Roll out thinly and use to line an 8-inch round loose-bottomed tart pan. Chill 30 minutes.

Preheat the oven to 400°F.

Bake the shell "blind" until lightly browned at the edge and cooked on the bottom, 10–15 minutes. Reduce the oven temperature to 350°F.

While the shell is baking make the filling: Mix the garlic, herbs, and cheese in a bowl until well blended. Stir in the yogurt, eggs, salt, and pepper and mix well. Pour the mixture into the pastry shell and return it to the cooler oven to bake until the filling has set, 20–25 minutes. Serve warm or cold.

ONION AND SAGE TART⋆

SERVES 6

FOR THE PASTRY
1 ¼ cups flour
½ tsp salt
¼ cup shortening, cut into small pieces
4 tbsp butter or margarine, cut into small pieces

FOR THE FILLING
¾ lb pearl or other tiny onions, unpeeled
2 tbsp butter
15 cherry tomatoes
2 tbsp chopped fresh sage
1 tbsp flour
⅔ cup vegetable stock
½ cup light cream
2 eggs, beaten
(⋆see page 2 for advice on eggs)
½ tsp salt and ¼ tsp freshly ground black pepper

FOR THE TOPPING
1 tbsp freshly grated Parmesan cheese
1 tbsp chopped fresh sage

To make the pastry: Sift the flour and salt into a bowl, add the shortening and butter or margarine, and rub them in finely with your fingertips. Stir in 2 tablespoons of cold water and mix together with a fork to form a firm dough.

Knead the dough on a lightly floured surface until smooth. Roll it out thinly and use to line a 9-inch round loose-bottomed tart pan. Chill 30 minutes.

Preheat the oven to 400°F.

Bake the pastry shell "blind" until lightly browned at the edges and cooked on the bottom, 10–15 minutes.

While the shell is baking make the filling: Place the onions in a saucepan and cover with cold water. Bring to a boil, cover, and cook until tender, about 10 minutes. Drain and cover with cold water. Drain again and then peel off the onion skins.

Melt the butter in a saucepan over medium-high heat. Add the peeled onions, the tomatoes, and sage and cook quickly for 1–2 minutes, shaking the saucepan constantly. Using a slotted spoon, transfer the tomatoes and onions to a plate. Let cool slightly, then cut them in half. Arrange them in the pastry shell.

Add the flour to the juices in the saucepan and stir well. Add the vegetable stock, bring to a boil, and cook 1 minute. Remove the saucepan from the heat and stir in the cream, eggs, salt, and pepper.

Pour the mixture into the pastry shell and return it to the oven to bake 15 minutes. Remove from the oven and give the tart its topping: Sprinkle the top with Parmesan cheese and sage. Continue baking until the filling has set and is golden brown, 10–15 minutes. Serve hot or cold.

Left: Fresh Herb and Garlic Tart; right: Onion and Sage Tart

TRADITIONAL TARTS

Many regions have their own time-honored tart recipes that have been passed down from generation to generation. Some, like Bakewell Tart or Yorkshire Curd Tart, are so delicious that they have become firm favorites all over the world. However, some of the recipes I have created for this chapter are my own very special adaptations of old favorites, like the Kentish Strawberry Tart, based on the strawberry trifle traditional in that part of the country, or the Highland Tart, which incorporates the popular Scottish oatmeal and cream dessert, Atholl Brose.

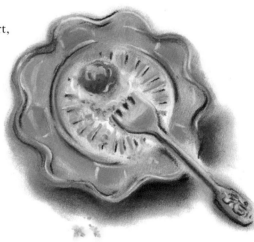

Left: Mincemeat and Orange Tart (page 34); right: Highland Tart (page 34)

GOLDEN
RASPBERRIES *are
well worth looking
for, not only for
their color but also
the fine flavor.*

OATS *ground into a
meal (fine, medium,
or coarse) are much
used in British
cooking,
particularly in
Scotland. If you
cannot find
medium-ground
oatmeal, grind
rolled oats to the
texture of coarse
cornmeal.*

HIGHLAND TART

SERVES 6

FOR THE PASTRY
¾ cup flour
¼ cup toasted and finely chopped hazelnuts
6 tbsp butter or margarine, cut into small pieces
2 tbsp sugar
1 egg yolk
FOR THE FILLING
1 cup heavy cream
3–4 tbsp Scotch whisky
2 tbsp honey
½ cup medium-ground oatmeal, toasted
1½ cups mixed golden and red raspberries
1¼ cups blueberries
3 tbsp quince or apple jelly, melted

To make the pastry: Sift the flour into a bowl, stir in the hazelnuts, add the butter or margarine, and rub it in finely with your fingertips. Stir in the sugar, egg yolk, and 1 tablespoon of cold water and mix together with a fork to form a firm dough.

Knead the dough on a lightly floured surface until smooth. Roll it out thinly and use to line an 8-inch round loose-bottomed fluted tart pan. Chill 30 minutes.

Preheat the oven to 400°F.

Bake the pastry shell "blind" until lightly browned at the edge and cooked on the bottom, 15–20 minutes.

While the shell is cooling make the filling: Place the cream, whisky, and honey in a bowl and whisk together until they are the consistency of thick cream. Fold in the oatmeal until evenly mixed.

Spread the oatmeal mixture over the bottom of the pastry shell and arrange the fruit on top. Brush the fruit with the quince or apple jelly glaze and let set.

MINCEMEAT AND ORANGE TART

SERVES 6

FOR THE PASTRY
1¼ cups flour
6 tbsp butter, cut into small pieces
2 tbsp sugar
2 tsp finely grated zest from a washed orange
FOR THE FILLING
½ cup mincemeat
2 washed seedless oranges
¾ cup sugar
2 tbsp Grand Marnier or Cointreau

To make the pastry: Sift the flour into a bowl, add the butter, and rub it in finely with your fingertips. Stir in the sugar, orange zest, and 2–3 tablespoons of cold water and mix together to a firm dough.

Knead the dough on a lightly floured surface until smooth. Roll it out thinly and use to line a 14-×4-inch rectangular loose-bottomed tart pan or form set on a baking sheet. Chill 30 minutes.

Preheat the oven to 400°F.

To make the filling: Spread the mincemeat evenly in the pastry shell and bake until the pastry is golden brown, 30–35 minutes.

Meanwhile, plunge the oranges into boiling water to blanch the skins, 1 minute. Let cool and then slice thinly.

Put the sugar in a frying pan with 1 cup of water and stir until the sugar has dissolved. Add the orange slices and simmer over low heat until the rind is tender and translucent, 15–20 minutes.

Remove the orange slices using a slotted spoon, cut the slices in half, and arrange them over the mincemeat filling. Sprinkle with the liqueur.

Boil the juice remaining in the pan until it becomes syrupy, 2–3 minutes. Spoon the syrup over the oranges to glaze. Let cool.

HARLEQUIN TART

SERVES 6

FOR THE PASTRY
1 ¼ cups flour
1 stick butter or margarine, cut into small pieces
1 tbsp sugar
FOR THE FILLING
6 tbsp apricot preserves
6 tbsp lemon and lime marmalade
6 tbsp raspberry preserves

To make the pastry: Sift the flour into a bowl, add the butter or margarine and rub it in finely with fingertips. Stir in the sugar and 3–4 tablespoons of cold water and mix together with a fork to form a firm dough.

Knead the dough on a lightly floured surface until smooth. Roll it out thinly and use to line an 8-inch square loose-bottomed fluted tart pan, reserving the pastry trimmings. Chill 30 minutes.

Preheat the oven to 400°F.

Using a skewer or toothpick, lightly mark on the bottom of the pastry shell two diagonal lines connecting opposite corners. Then mark another two lines joining the mid-points of opposite edges of the pastry shell, dividing the shell into 8 triangles. Mark 4 more lines across the corners of the pastry shell, connecting mid-points of adjacent sides, to form 16 triangles in all.

Carefully fill each triangle with one of the preserves or the marmalade, alternating the colors and flavors. Spread each layer evenly.

Knead the pastry trimmings together and roll out to a thin oblong. Cut into thin strips and lay the strips across the tart to separate the jam triangles. Trim all the strips to fit.

Bake until the pastry is pale golden in color, 15–20 minutes. Serve warm or cold.

If the jams in the HARLEQUIN TART *recipe are not available, simply use a mixture of different colored jams such as strawberry, plum, greengage, cherry, and blueberry.*

Harlequin Tart

MALVERN TART *is a recipe devised from Malvern Pudding, a dessert that originated in Worcestershire. A sweet sauce was topped with sugar and spices and then baked until golden. Apples, being plentiful in the Malvern area, were added to the recipe to give a variation.*

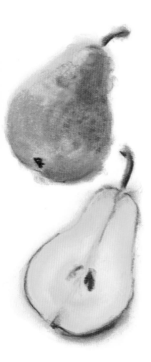

MALVERN TART

SERVES 6

FOR THE PASTRY

1 ¼ cups flour

1 stick butter or margarine, cut into small pieces

2 tbsp sugar

1 egg yolk

FOR THE FILLING

4 tbsp butter

5 tbsp sugar

4 pears, peeled and thinly sliced

1 quince or apple, peeled, cored, and thinly sliced

2 tbsp flour

2 cups milk

1 bay leaf

FOR THE TOPPING

⅓ cup raw or light brown sugar

½ tsp ground cinnamon

To make the pastry: Sift the flour into a bowl, add the butter or margarine, and rub it in finely with your fingertips. Stir in the sugar, egg yolk, and 2–3 tablespoons of cold water and mix together with a fork to form a firm dough.

Knead on a lightly floured surface until smooth. Roll it out thinly and use to line a 9-inch round tart or quiche dish. Chill 30 minutes.

Preheat the oven to 400°F.

Bake the pastry shell "blind" until lightly browned and cooked on the bottom, 15–20 minutes.

While the shell is baking make the filling: Melt half the butter with half the sugar in a saucepan over heat. Add the pears and quince or apple and cook rapidly, stirring occasionally, until the fruit is tender and the juice has turned syrupy. Pour the contents of the pan into the pastry shell.

Place the remaining butter and sugar, the flour, milk, and bay leaf in the pan. Whisking constantly over medium heat, bring to a boil. Simmer until the sauce is thick and smooth, 1–2 minutes. Remove the bay leaf and pour the sauce over the fruit in the pastry shell. Let cool so that the sauce sets on top.

To make the tart topping: Preheat the broiler. Mix together the sugar and cinnamon. Sprinkle this over the tart filling and broil until the sugar has caramelized. Serve hot or cold.

DUKE OF CAMBRIDGE TART

SERVES 4–6

FOR THE PASTRY

¾ cup flour

4 tbsp butter or margarine, cut into small pieces

2 tsp sugar

2–3 tbsp lemon juice

FOR THE FILLING

2 tbsp quince or apple jelly

finely grated zest and 1 tbsp juice from a washed lemon

1 tbsp chopped candied peel

¾ cup chopped mixed candied fruits

6 tbsp self-rising flour

½ tsp baking powder

5 tbsp sugar

4 tbsp butter or margarine, softened

1 egg

FOR DECORATION

confectioners' sugar

To make the pastry: Sift the flour, add the butter or margarine and rub it in finely with your fingertips. Stir in the sugar and lemon juice and mix together with a fork to form a firm dough.

Knead the dough on a lightly floured surface until smooth. Roll it out thinly and use to line an 8-inch round tart or quiche dish. Chill about 30 minutes. Preheat the oven to 325°F.

Duke of Cambridge Tart

To make the filling: Spread the quince or apple jelly over the bottom of the shell. In a bowl mix together the lemon zest and juice, candied peel, and two-thirds of the chopped mixed candied fruits.

Sift the flour and baking powder into a bowl. Add the sugar, butter or margarine, and egg. Beat with a wooden spoon until light and fluffy, 1–2 minutes. Stir in the mixed fruit until well blended. Spread the filling evenly over the bottom of the pastry shell.

Bake until the filling is well risen, golden brown, and firm to the touch in the center, 40–45 minutes.

Dust the top with confectioners' sugar and decorate with the remaining chopped mixed candied fruits. Serve hot, warm, or cold.

NORFOLK TREACLE TART

SERVES 8

FOR THE PASTRY
1 ¼ cups flour
1 stick butter, cut into small pieces
1 tbsp lemon juice
FOR THE FILLING
⅔ cup golden syrup
2 tbsp butter
6 tbsp light cream
2 eggs, beaten
grated zest and juice from 1 washed lemon
1 ⅓ cups fresh white bread crumbs

To make the pastry: Sift the flour into a bowl, add the butter, and rub it in finely with your fingertips. Stir in the lemon juice and 2 tablespoons of cold water and mix together with a fork to form a firm dough.

Knead the dough on a lightly floured surface until smooth. Roll it out thinly and use to line a 9-inch round tart or quiche dish, reserving the pastry trimmings. Chill 30 minutes.

Preheat the oven to 400°F.

To make the filling: Place the golden syrup in a saucepan and heat gently until liquid. Remove the pan from the heat, add the butter, and stir until melted. Then beat in the cream, eggs, lemon zest, and juice until well blended.

Sprinkle the bread crumbs over the bottom of the pastry shell and pour the syrup mixture over the top. Roll out the pastry trimmings, cut into thin strips, and use to make a lattice design over the top.

Bake until the pastry is golden brown and the filling has set, 40–45 minutes. Let cool and serve warm or cold.

Clockwise from the top: Fruit Bakewell Tart; Rum and Butterscotch Tart (page 40); Norfolk Treacle Tart

FRUIT BAKEWELL TART

SERVES 6

FOR THE PASTRY
¾ cup flour
4 tbsp butter or margarine, cut into small pieces
1 tsp sugar
FOR THE FILLING
3 tbsp red currant jelly
½ cup each red currants, white currants, and black currants
6 tbsp butter or margarine, softened
7 tbsp sugar
⅔ cup ground almonds
6 tbsp self-rising flour
2 eggs, beaten
1 tsp almond extract
⅓ cup sliced almonds
FOR DECORATION
confectioners' sugar

Make the pastry: Sift flour into a bowl, add the butter or margarine, and rub in finely. Stir in the sugar and 2 tablespoons of cold water. Mix to a firm dough. Knead until smooth. Roll out thinly and use to line an 8-inch round loose-bottomed fluted tart pan. Chill 30 minutes. Preheat the oven to 350°F.

To make the filling: Spread the red currant jelly over the bottom of the shell. Reserve a few stems of each type of fruit, and remove the remainder from their stems. Scatter over the jelly.

Beat together the butter or margarine, sugar, ground almonds, flour, eggs, and almond extract 1–2 minutes. Spread this mixture over the fruit in the pastry shell. Scatter the sliced almonds evenly over the top and bake until the filling has risen and feels firm when pressed lightly in the center.

Cool in the pan, then remove carefully. Dust with confectioners' sugar and decorate with the reserved fruit.

GOLDEN SYRUP
can be found in some supermarkets and many specialty markets. You can substitute corn syrup or light molasses.

BAKEWELL TART *is named after the town of Bakewell in Derbyshire. The layers were traditionally separated by crushed raspberries or raspberry preserves, to add moisture.*

KENTISH
STRAWBERRY
TART *consists of a*
strawberry trifle
enclosed in a light,
crisp almond pastry.
Trifles were very
popular in
Victorian England.
They were made
using light sponge
cakes soaked in
sherry, brandy, or
Madeira, layered
with fruit – Kentish
strawberries being
the most popular –
and covered with a
rich egg custard
sauce.

RUM AND BUTTERSCOTCH TART

SERVES 6

FOR THE PASTRY
1¼ cups flour
1 stick butter
2 tbsp sugar
1 egg

FOR THE FILLING
½ cup packed dark brown sugar
4 tbsp butter
¼ cup flour
1¼ cups milk
⅔ cup light cream
2–3 tbsp dark rum

FOR DECORATION
whipped cream
chocolate-coated coffee beans

To make the pastry: Sift the flour into a bowl, add the butter, and rub it in finely with your fingertips. Stir in the sugar and egg and mix together with a fork to form a firm dough.

Knead the dough on a lightly floured surface until smooth. Roll it out thinly and use to line a 9-inch round tart or quiche dish. Chill 30 minutes.

Preheat the oven to 400°F.

Bake the pastry shell "blind" until lightly browned at the edges and cooked at the base, 15–20 minutes.

While the shell is cooling make the filling: Place the sugar, butter, flour, milk, and cream in a saucepan. Whisking constantly over medium heat; bring to a boil. Simmer until the sauce is thick and smooth, 1–2 minutes. Stir in the rum.

Pour the filling into the pastry shell and leave until cold. Decorate the top with whipped cream and chocolate-coated coffee beans.

KENTISH STRAWBERRY TART

SERVES 8

FOR THE PASTRY
¾ cup flour
⅔ cup ground almonds
1 stick butter, cut into small pieces
2 tbsp sugar
1 tsp almond extract
1 egg

FOR THE FILLING
1 egg + 1 extra yolk
1 tsp pure vanilla extract
2½ tbsp sugar
3 tbsp flour
1¼ cups milk
3 tbsp strawberry preserves
10 ladyfingers, cut in half
2 tbsp Madeira wine
1½–2 cups strawberries, sliced
1¼ cups whipping cream, whipped

FOR DECORATION
strawberry slices and strawberry leaves

Make the pastry: Sift the flour into a bowl, stir in the almonds, add the butter, and rub in finely. Stir in the sugar, almond extract, and egg and mix to a firm dough.

Knead the dough until smooth. Roll it out thinly and use to line a 11-×7-inch rectangular fluted tart or quiche dish. Chill 30 minutes.

Preheat the oven to 400°F.

Bake the pastry shell "blind" until lightly browned at the edges, 15–20 minutes.

While the shell is baking, make the filling: In a bowl whisk together the egg, egg yolk, vanilla extract, sugar, and flour until well blended. Place the milk in a saucepan and bring it to a boil. Whisking constantly, pour the milk over the egg mixture. Return to the pan and continue whisking over low heat until the custard thickens. Let cool.

Spread the jam in the pastry shell. Dip the ladyfingers into the Madeira, turning to coat well. Arrange them over the jam. Cover with strawberry slices.

Fold two-thirds of the whipped cream into the custard and spread evenly over the strawberries.

Place the remaining cream in a pastry bag fitted with a small star tip. Pipe ropes of cream across the tart and decorate with strawberry slices and leaves.

IRISH APPLE TART

SERVES 6

FOR THE PASTRY
½ cup + 2 tbsp flour
2 tbsp butter, cut into small pieces
1 tsp sugar
½ lb baking potatoes, cooked and puréed
FOR THE FILLING
1½ lb apples, cored, peeled, and thinly sliced
2½ tbsp sugar
1 tsp ground cloves
⅔ cup sour cream
2 tsp honey

To make the pastry: Place the flour in a bowl, add the butter, and rub it in finely with your fingertips. Stir in the sugar and potato and mix to a soft dough.

Roll out the dough thinly and use to line a 9-inch round tart or quiche dish.

Preheat the oven to 375°F.

Mix together the apples, sugar, and cloves and pile the mixture in the pastry shell. Bake until the apples are almost tender, 20–25 minutes.

Stir the apples, spread the sour cream over the top, and drizzle with honey. Bake until the cream has set, 5–10 minutes longer. Serve warm or cold.

Kentish Strawberry Tart

FRUIT TARTS

Fruit tarts are among the most popular and eye-catching of pastries. They are a very appealing way of serving the bounties of the summer fruit season and are usually fairly simple in that only the pastry shell is baked. Often with no more than a layer of custard or flavored cream beneath the fruit, they are usually finished with a coating of fruit glaze over the fruit to hold it in place and help keep it fresh.

The French often make their fruit tarts in the long rectangular "tranche" form, so called because the finished pastry then lends itself to being sliced across into rectangular pieces for easier serving.

Chopped nuts, tiny mint sprigs, or a light dusting of confectioners' sugar are the most usual decorations.

Clockwise from the top: Peach and Passion Fruit Tart (page 44); Plum and Sour Cream Tart (page 44); Minted Currant Tart (page 45)

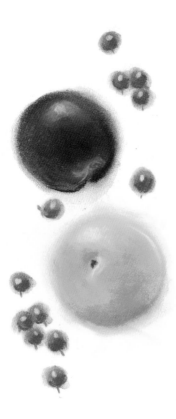

PLUM AND SOUR CREAM TART

SERVES 6

FOR THE PASTRY
1 ¼ cups flour
1 stick butter, cut into small pieces
2 tbsp sugar
3 tbsp sour cream
FOR THE FILLING
⅔ cup crushed amaretti cookies
¼ cup sour cream
¼ cup packed light brown sugar
½ lb red plums, halved
½ lb yellow plums, halved
¼ cup red currant jelly

To make the pastry: Sift the flour into a bowl, add the butter, and rub it in finely with your fingertips. Stir in the sugar and sour cream and mix together with a fork to form a firm dough.

Knead the dough on a lightly floured surface until it is smooth. Roll it out thinly and use to line an 8-inch round loose-bottomed fluted tart pan, reserving the trimmings. Chill 30 minutes.

Preheat the oven to 375°F.

To make the filling: In a bowl, mix together the crushed cookies, sour cream, and brown sugar. Spread the mixture in the pastry shell and arrange the plums on top, alternating the colors.

Roll out the pastry trimmings thinly and cut out 12 thin strips. Arrange these over the plums in a lattice design. Trim off the ends and press the strips onto the edge of the pastry shell.

Bake until the pastry is lightly browned and the plums are tender, 35–40 minutes. Let cool.

Heat the red currant jelly until melted, then pour it in between the pastry lattice to glaze the plums. Let set.

PEACH AND PASSION FRUIT TART

SERVES 8

FOR THE PASTRY
1 ¼ cups flour
1 stick butter, cut into small pieces
2 tbsp sugar
1 egg
FOR THE FILLING
2 eggs
½ cup whipping cream
5 tbsp sugar
strained juice from 3 passion fruits
6 peaches, peeled and halved
¼ cup pistachio nuts, shelled
¼ cup apricot preserves, boiled and strained

To make the pastry: Sift the flour into a bowl, add the butter, and rub it in finely with your fingertips. Stir in the sugar and egg and mix together with a fork to form a firm dough.

Knead the dough on a lightly floured surface until it is smooth. Roll it out thinly and use to line a 9-inch round tart or quiche dish. Chill 30 minutes.

Preheat the oven to 400°F.

Bake the pastry shell "blind" until lightly browned at the edge and cooked on the bottom, 10–15 minutes. Reduce the oven temperature to 325°F.

While the shell is baking make the filling: Place the eggs, cream, sugar, and passion fruit juice in a bowl. Beat together until well blended.

Pour the mixture into the pastry shell and return it to the oven to bake until the filling has set, 30–40 minutes. Let cool.

Arrange the peaches over the custard filling and decorate with pistachio nuts. Brush the top with the apricot preserves and let set.

MINTED CURRANT TART

SERVES 6

FOR THE PASTRY
¾ cup flour
6 tbsp butter, cut into small pieces
2 tbsp sugar
1 egg yolk
FOR THE FILLING
2½ cups red currants
2½ cups white currants
2 sprigs of fresh mint
¼ cup cornstarch
½ cup + 1 tbsp sugar
FOR DECORATION
sprigs of fresh mint

To make the pastry: Sift the flour into a bowl, add the butter, and rub in finely with your fingertips. Stir in the sugar and egg yolk and mix to a firm dough.

Knead the dough until it is smooth. Roll it out thinly and use to line an 8-inch round loose-bottomed fluted tart pan. Chill 30 minutes.

Preheat the oven to 400°F.

Bake the pastry shell "blind" until lightly browned at the edges, 15–20 minutes.

While the shell is baking make the filling: Place half each of the red currants and white currants with the mint in a saucepan with 1 cup of water. Bring to a boil and simmer 2 minutes. Pour the pan contents into a strainer set over a bowl and rub through the fruit, discarding the stems and seeds.

Blend the cornstarch with ¼ cup of water in a saucepan. Add the strained fruit purée, stir well, and bring to a boil. Let cool 5 minutes, then stir in the sugar and pour the mixture into the pastry shell. Leave until cold.

Decorate the top of the tart with the remaining red currants and white currants and mint sprigs.

TARTE FRANÇAISE

SERVES 8

¾ lb frozen puff pastry, thawed
FOR THE FILLING
6 tbsp apricot preserves, boiled and strained
6 oz cream cheese
3 tbsp plain yogurt
1 tbsp honey
i tsp pure vanilla extract
1 lb mixed soft fruits, such as cherries, raspberries, strawberries, apricots, peaches, plums, pitted and sliced as necessary

Roll out the pastry on a lightly floured surface to make an oblong about 12×8 inches. Lightly flour the pastry surface and then fold the pastry in half lengthwise to make a long narrow oblong.

Measure 1 inch down from the top of one narrow edge and cut across the fold to within 1 inch of the open edge. Repeat at the bottom.

Cut a line 1 inch in from the open edge to join up with the side cuts. Remove the center piece from the "frame," open out the pastry, and roll out and trim to match the size of the pastry frame.

Place the oblong on a dampened baking sheet, brush the edges with water, and place the frame on top. Press the edges together to seal well. Cut up the edges with a knife to form flakes. Mark a design on the top of the edges. Prick the bottom and chill 30 minutes.

Meanwhile, preheat the oven to 425°F.

Bake the pastry shell until risen and golden brown, 15–20 minutes. Cool on a wire rack and then brush the bottom with some apricot preserves.

Beat the cream cheese, yogurt, honey, and vanilla together in a bowl until well blended. Spread the mixture evenly in the pastry shell and cover with an arrangement of soft fruits. Brush well with the remaining preserves and let set.

Citrus Tart

KUMQUAT-FRANGIPANE TART

SERVES 6

FOR THE PASTRY
¾ cup flour
6 tbsp butter, cut into small pieces
2 tbsp sugar
1 egg yolk
FOR THE FILLING
6 tbsp butter, softened
1 ¼ cups sugar
1 egg + 1 extra yolk
1 cup ground almonds
1 tbsp cornstarch
1 tsp almond extract
¼ cup apricot preserves
6 oz kumquats, sliced

To make the pastry: Sift the flour into a bowl, add the butter, and rub it in finely with your fingertips. Stir in the sugar and egg yolk and mix together with a fork to form a firm dough.

Knead the dough lightly on a floured surface until it is smooth. Roll it out thinly and use to line a 14-×4-inch rectangular loose-bottomed tart pan or form set on a baking sheet. Chill 30 minutes.

Preheat the oven to 400°F.

Bake the pastry "blind" until lightly browned at the edges and cooked on the bottom, about 10 minutes. Reduce the oven temperature to 350°F.

While the shell is baking make the filling: Place the butter and one-third of the sugar in a bowl and beat them together with a wooden spoon until light and fluffy. Gradually add the egg and egg yolk, beating well after each addition. Fold in the ground almonds, cornstarch, and almond extract until evenly mixed.

Spread the apricot preserves over the bottom of the pastry shell and spoon the almond mixture on top, spreading it evenly. Bake in the cooler oven until the filling is well risen, golden brown, and firm to the touch in the center, 45–50 minutes. Let it cool slightly before removing it from the pan.

Place the remaining sugar and 1 cup of water in a saucepan and heat gently, stirring occasionally, until the sugar has dissolved. Add the kumquat slices, bring to a boil, and simmer until they are translucent, 2–3 minutes.

Using a slotted spoon, remove the kumquats from the syrup and arrange over the top of the tart. Boil the syrup until the surface is covered in bubbles, then pour over the kumquats. Let cool and set.

CITRUS TART

SERVES 6

FOR THE PASTRY
1 cup flour
6 tbsp butter, cut into small pieces
2 tbsp sugar
2 egg yolks
FOR THE FILLING
finely grated zest and juice of 2 washed limes
finely grated zest and juice of 1 washed orange
finely grated zest and juice of 1 washed lemon
3 eggs+1 extra yolk
½ cup+1 tbsp sugar
⅔ cup whipping cream
FOR THE TOPPING
1 orange
1 lemon
1 lime
¾ cup sugar

To make the pastry: Sift the flour into a bowl, add the butter, and rub it in finely with your fingertips.

Stir in the sugar and egg yolks and mix together with a fork to form a firm dough.

Knead the dough on a lightly floured surface until it is smooth. Roll it out thinly and use to line a 9½-inch round loose-bottomed fluted tart pan. Chill 30 minutes.

Preheat the oven to 400°F.

Bake the pastry shell "blind" until lightly browned at the edge and cooked at the base, 10–15 minutes. Reduce the oven temperature to 325°F.

While the shell is baking make the filling: Measure ¾ cup of mixed fruit juice, adding some water if necessary. Whisk together the eggs, egg yolk, sugar, and cream until well blended. Stir in the measured juice and the zest, mix well, and pour into the pastry shell.

Bake in the cooler oven until the filling has just set, 50–55 minutes. Let cool in the pan before removing.

Make the topping: Peel the fruits with a sharp knife, making sure that all the white pith is removed. Slice the fruits thinly.

Place the sugar in a saucepan with ⅔ cup of water. Heat gently, stirring occasionally, until the sugar has dissolved. Add the lemon and lime slices to the syrup and bring to a boil. Using a slotted spoon, remove the fruit slices from the syrup and arrange them with the orange slices over the tart.

Boil the syrup 1–2 minutes, until the surface is covered with bubbles. Pour it over the tart and let cool.

The term FRANGIPANE *was first used in the 18th century for pâtisserie fillings flavored with almond extract and orange flower water.*

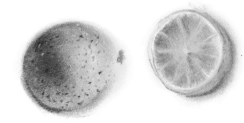

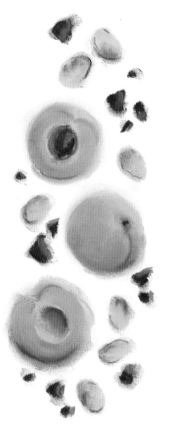

APRICOT-CHOCOLATE TART

SERVES 6

FOR THE PASTRY
1¼ cups flour
1 stick butter, cut into small pieces
2 tbsp sugar
1 tsp almond extract
1 egg

FOR THE FILLING
2 egg yolks
7 tbsp sugar
¼ cup flour
1¼ cups milk
1 oz semisweet chocolate
¼ cup whipping cream
1 lb apricots, halved
2½ tbsp sliced almonds, toasted
¼ cup apricot preserves

To make the pastry: Sift the flour into a bowl, add the butter, and rub it in finely with your fingertips. Stir in the sugar, almond extract, and egg and mix together with a fork to form a firm dough.

Knead the dough on a lightly floured surface until it is smooth. Roll it out thinly and use to line a 9-inch round loose-bottomed fluted tart pan. Chill 30 minutes.

Preheat the oven to 400°F.

Bake the pastry shell "blind" until lightly browned at the edges, 15–20 minutes.

While the shell is baking make the filling: In a bowl, whisk together the egg yolks, 2 tablespoons of the sugar, the flour, and 1 tablespoon of the measured milk until smooth. In a saucepan, bring the remaining milk and the chocolate to a boil, whisking, then pour over the egg mixture, whisking constantly over low heat. Return the mixture to the saucepan and cook gently, whisking well, until the custard has thickened. Remove the saucepan

from the heat and whisk in the cream. Pour the custard into the pastry shell and leave until cold.

Place the remaining sugar in a saucepan with ⅓ cup of water and bring to a boil, stirring. Add the apricot halves, cover, and cook gently until tender, 2–3 minutes. Using a slotted spoon, remove the apricots from the syrup and arrange them over the custard filling. Scatter the almonds on top.

Add the apricot preserves to the syrup in the saucepan and bring to a boil. Boil 1 minute, then strain into a bowl. Let cool slightly.

Pour the apricot syrup evenly over the apricots to glaze and then let cool.

PRUNE AND ARMAGNAC TART

SERVES 6

FOR THE PASTRY
¾ cup flour
6 tbsp butter, cut into small pieces
2 tbsp sugar
1 egg yolk

FOR THE FILLING
20 plump pitted prunes
¼ cup Armagnac or brandy
1 tbsp honey
1 tbsp light brown sugar
½ cup whipping cream
2 eggs
3 tbsp hazelnuts, halved

FOR DECORATION
confectioners' sugar

To make the pastry: Sift the flour into a bowl, add the butter, and rub it in finely with your fingertips. Stir in the sugar and egg yolk and mix together with a fork to form a firm dough.

Knead the dough on a lightly floured surface until it is smooth. Roll it out thinly and use to line an 8-inch round loose-bottomed fluted tart pan. Chill 30 minutes. Preheat the oven to 400°F.

Bake the pastry shell "blind" until lightly browned at the edge and cooked on the bottom, 10–15 minutes.

While the shell is baking make the filling: Place the prunes and Armagnac or brandy in a small saucepan and warm gently over low heat, taking care not to over-heat. Cover and leave until cold.

Beat the honey, sugar, cream, and eggs together until well blended. Strain the Armagnac or brandy into the mixture and place the prunes in the shell.

Stir the filling, pour it over the prunes, and return the tart to the oven to bake 20 minutes. Scatter the hazelnuts over the top and continue baking until the filling has set, about 10 minutes longer. Dust with confectioners' sugar and serve warm or cold.

ROSÉ PEAR TART

SERVES 6

FOR THE PASTRY
¾ cup flour
6 tbsp butter, cut into small pieces
½ cup finely chopped walnuts
2 tbsp sugar
1 egg
FOR THE FILLING
1¼ cups rosé wine
1 cup sugar
5 small pears, peeled, quartered, and cored
2 egg yolks
¼ cup flour
1 tbsp rose water
1¼ cups milk
¼ cup whipping cream
2 tsp unflavored gelatin

To make the pastry: Sift the flour into a bowl, add the butter, and rub it in finely with your fingertips. Stir in the walnuts, sugar, and egg and mix together with a fork to form a firm dough.

Knead the dough until smooth. Roll it out thinly and use to line an 8-inch square loose-bottomed fluted tart pan. Chill 30 minutes.

Preheat the oven to 400°F.

Bake the pastry shell "blind" until lightly browned at the edges, 15–20 minutes.

While the shell is baking make the filling: Place the wine and ¾ cup of the sugar in a pan and heat gently, stirring, until the sugar has dissolved. Add the pears and bring to a boil. Cover and cook over low heat until tender, 10–15 minutes. Let cool.

In a bowl, whisk together the egg yolks, remaining sugar, the flour, and rose water until smooth. Bring the milk to a boil in a saucepan and pour it over the egg mixture, whisking all the time. Return the mixture to the saucepan and cook over low heat, whisking well, until the custard has thickened. Remove from the heat and whisk in the cream. Pour into the pastry shell and let cool.

Using a slotted spoon, transfer the pears to a large plate. Blend the gelatin with 2 tablespoons of water and stir this into the wine syrup until dissolved. Leave until almost set.

Meanwhile, cut half of the pear quarters into about 4 thin slices each, keeping the quarters together with the rounded sides on the right hand side. Slice the remaining pear quarters in the same way, with the rounded sides on the left.

Arrange 5 of the pear quarters on the custard filling and press lightly to spread them evenly; place another 5 quarters cut in the other direction and spread similarly. Repeat the process with the remaining pear halves in different directions.

When the gelatin has begun to set, spoon it over the pears and chill until set. Remove from the pan for serving.

ROSEMARY TARTE TATIN

SERVES 8

½ lb frozen puff pastry, thawed
butter, for greasing
FOR THE FILLING
1 stick unsalted butter
¾ cup sugar
2 tbsp honey
6 apples, peeled, quartered, and cored
finely grated zest of 1 washed lemon
2 tbsp fresh rosemary leaves

On a lightly floured surface roll out the puff pastry to an 8-inch round and place this on a large plate. Prick all over with a fork and chill until the filling is ready. Grease an 8-inch round layer cake pan with butter and line the bottom with wax paper.

To make the filling: Place the butter, sugar, and honey in a nonstick frying pan and cook over low heat, stirring occasionally, until lightly browned and syrupy.

Add the apples, lemon zest, and rosemary to the syrup and cook over medium heat, stirring and turning the apples in the syrup, until tender.

Using a slotted spoon, transfer the apples to the prepared pan. Boil the syrup until thick and bubbly, 1–2 minutes. Strain over the apples and leave until cold.

Preheat the oven to 400°F. Place the pastry round over the filling in the pan and bake until the pastry is golden brown, about 20 minutes. Let cool in the pan 15 minutes, then invert onto a serving plate with a rim and remove the paper. Serve hot or warm.

Clockwise from the top: Normandy Apple Tart (page 52); Rosemary Tarte Tatin; Rosé Pear Tart (page 49)

TARTE TATIN *is named after "Les demoiselles Tatin," the Tatin sisters, who were the local hotel-keepers at Lamotte–Beuvron in the Sologne area of France's Loire Valley. It was their specialty and was arguably the first upside-down apple tart. The sisters cooked the tart in a metal oven heated with charcoal, which gave the dish its characteristic caramelized buttery apples and light, crisp pastry.*

NORMANDY APPLE TART

SERVES 6

FOR THE PASTRY
1 cup flour
6 tbsp butter, cut into small pieces
2 tbsp sugar
2 egg yolks
FOR THE FILLING
1 stick unsalted butter, softened
½ cup + 2 tbsp sugar
3 egg yolks
2 tbsp whipping cream
1¼ cups ground almonds
2 tbsp crumbled lavender flowers
4 apples, peeled, halved, and cored
¼ cup apricot preserves, boiled and strained

Normandy, being the apple-growing region of France, strongly features apples in its traditional cooking. There are many variations of this tart and the addition of the sweet scent of lavender is particularly rewarding.

Make the pastry: Sift flour into a bowl, add the butter, and rub in finely with your fingertips. Stir in the sugar and egg yolks and mix to a firm dough.

Knead until smooth. Roll it out thinly and use to line a 9-inch round loose-bottomed fluted tart pan. Chill 30 minutes. Preheat the oven to 400°F.

To make the filling: In a bowl, beat together the butter and ½ cup of the sugar until light and fluffy. Add the egg yolks one at a time, beating well after each. Stir in the cream and fold in the almonds.

Scatter the lavender over the bottom of the pastry shell. Then spread the almond mixture over these.

Slice the apple halves very thinly, keeping the halves together. Place one half in the center of the filling and arrange the remaining 7 evenly around it. Press each apple half gently to spread out the slices.

Bake 15 minutes, then sprinkle the remaining sugar over the apples. Reduce the oven temperature to 350°F and continue baking until the filling is lightly browned, 40–45 minutes longer.

Let cool before removing the tart from the pan. Brush the top evenly with the apricot preserves.

ROSE CUSTARD TARTLETS

MAKES 8

FOR THE PASTRY
¾ cup flour
6 tbsp butter or margarine, cut into small pieces
⅔ cup ground almonds
5 tbsp sugar
1 egg, beaten
FOR THE FILLING
2 eggs + 2 extra yolks
2 tbsp rose water
1 tbsp flour
¾ cup milk
1¼ cups light cream
1 pint wild strawberries or pitted cherries

To make the pastry: Sift the flour into a bowl. Add the butter or margarine and rub it in finely with your fingertips. Stir in the ground almonds, sugar, and egg and mix with a fork to form a firm dough.

Knead the dough on a lightly floured surface until it is smooth. Roll it out thinly, and use to line eight 4½-inch loose-bottomed fluted tartlet molds. Chill 30 minutes.

Preheat the oven to 400°F.

Bake the pastry shells "blind" until lightly browned at the edges, 10–15 minutes. Reduce the oven temperature to 350°F.

Place the eggs, egg yolks, rose water, and flour in a bowl and whisk until smooth. Whisk in the milk and cream and pour the mixture into the pastry shells. Dot with the fruit.

Return the tartlets to the cooler oven to bake until the filling has just set, 45–50 minutes. Let cool before serving.

A Rose Custard Tartlet

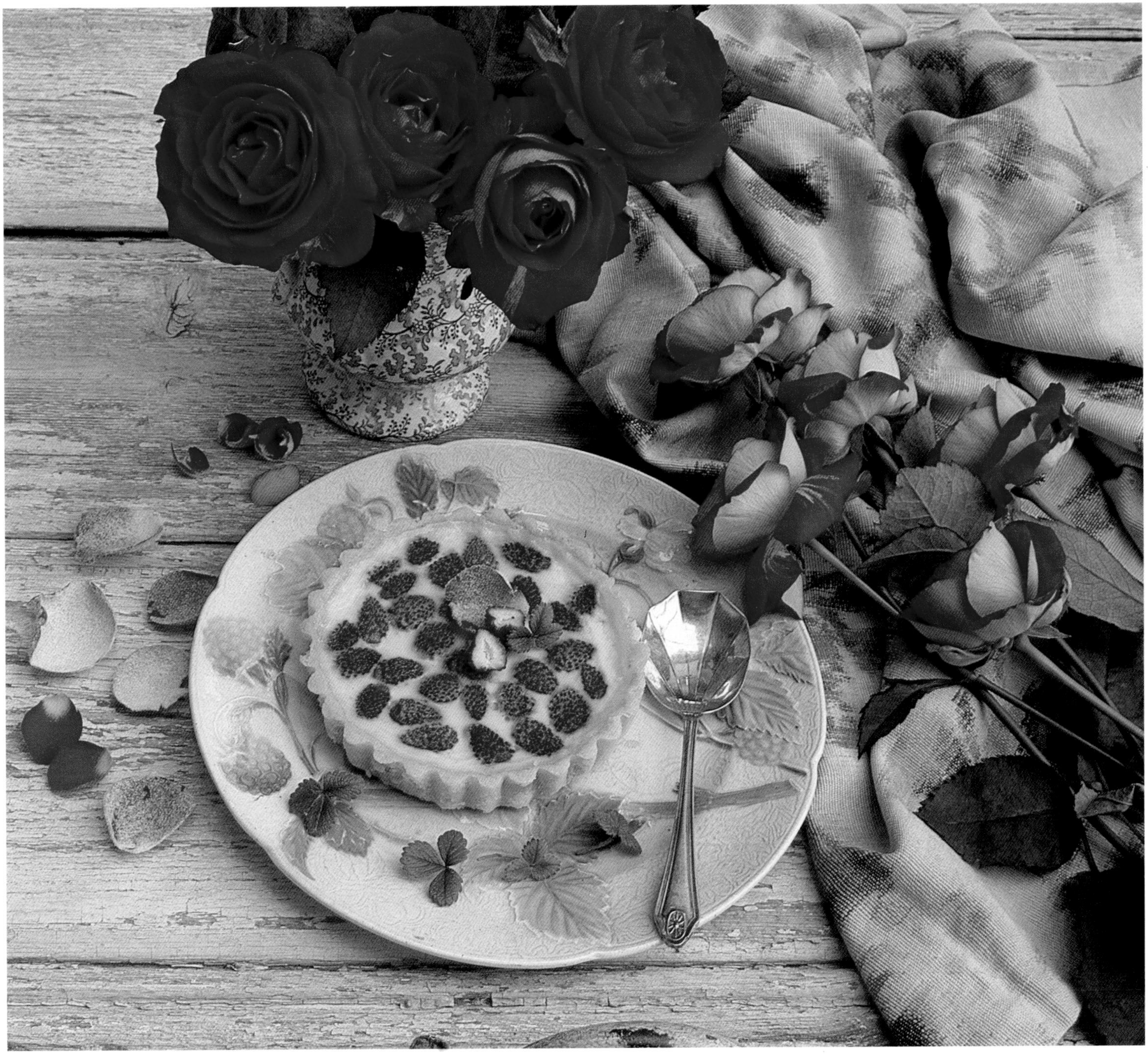

SWEET TARTS

An amalgamation of unusual textures and exciting flavor combinations characterizes the varied recipes in this chapter, from soft cheese and custard fillings studded with exotic crystallized fruits to tarts filled with chocolate mousse, mocha, and creamy chestnut mixtures. Again I have made some more unusual pastries by adapting recipes for traditional dishes, such as the Rhubarb and Ginger Cream Tart and the Orange Rice Tart, flavored like a Middle-Eastern rice pudding with bay leaves and orange flower water. Many of these tarts are decorated by piping whipped cream or melted chocolate attractively over the top.

Clockwise from the top left: Mocha-Walnut Tart (page 57); Chocolate Mousse Tart (page 56); Chestnut Tart (page 56); Pecan-Chocolate Tart (page 57)

CHOCOLATE MOUSSE TART★

SERVES 6

FOR THE PASTRY
1 ¼ cups flour
1 stick butter or margarine, cut into small pieces
2 tbsp sugar
1 egg yolk
FOR THE FILLING
6 oz semisweet chocolate
½ oz white chocolate
3 eggs, separated
(★see page 2 for advice on eggs)
2 tbsp dark rum

To make the pastry: Sift the flour into a bowl, add the butter or margarine and rub it in finely with your fingertips. Stir in the sugar, egg yolk, and 1 tablespoon of water and mix to a firm dough.

Knead the dough until it is smooth. Roll it out thinly and use to line a 14-×4-inch rectangular loose-bottomed fluted tart pan or form set on a baking sheet. Chill 30 minutes.

Preheat the oven to 400°F. Bake the shell "blind" until lightly browned at the edges, 15–20 minutes.

While the shell is cooling make the filling: Place the semisweet and white chocolate in separate clean, dry bowls over hot water. Stir occasionally until melted. Stir the egg yolks and rum into the semisweet chocolate until well blended and thick.

Beat the egg whites in a clean bowl until stiff. Gradually add the egg white to the semisweet chocolate mixture, folding it in gently.

Pour the semisweet chocolate mixture into the pastry shell and shake gently to level. Place the melted white chocolate in a paper piping cone, fold down the top, and snip off the point.

Pipe parallel lines of white chocolate across the chocolate filling. Draw a toothpick across the white chocolate lines to feather them. Let it set.

CHESTNUT TART

SERVES 6

FOR THE PASTRY
1 ¼ cups flour
6 tbsp butter or margarine, cut into small pieces
1 tbsp chocolate fudge sauce
FOR THE FILLING
15 oz canned unsweetened chestnut purée
1 cup cream cheese
2 tbsp Marsala wine
4 oz white chocolate, melted
⅔ cup light cream
2 oz semisweet chocolate, melted
FOR DECORATION
white and dark chocolate curls

To make the pastry: Sift the flour into a bowl, add the butter or margarine, and rub it in finely with your fingertips. Stir in the fudge sauce and 2–3 tablespoons of cold water and mix to a firm dough.

Knead the dough until it is smooth. Roll it out thinly and use to line a 9-inch round loose-bottomed fluted tart pan. Chill 30 minutes.

Preheat the oven to 400°F. Bake the pastry shell "blind" until lightly browned at the edges, 15–20 minutes. Let it cool on a wire rack.

While the shell is cooling make the filling: Place half the chestnut purée, the cheese, and Marsala in a food processor and process until smooth. Stir in the white chocolate until well blended.

Place the remaining chestnut purée and the cream in the food processor and process until smooth. Add the semisweet chocolate and blend well.

Spread half the semisweet chocolate mixture in the pastry shell and spread the white chocolate mixture over it.

Put the remaining semisweet chocolate mixture in a pastry bag fitted with a plain tip. Pipe a lattice on top and decorate with chocolate curls.

MOCHA-WALNUT TART

SERVES 6

FOR THE PASTRY

¾ cup flour

6 tbsp butter, cut into small pieces

½ cup finely chopped walnuts

2 tbsp light brown sugar

1 egg

FOR THE FILLING

1¼ cups milk

2 oz semisweet chocolate

4 tbsp unsalted butter

1 tsp instant coffee granules

1 tbsp cornstarch

2 egg yolks

2 tbsp Tia Maria

⅔ cup light cream

FOR DECORATION

⅔ cup whipping cream, whipped to soft peaks

chocolate-coated coffee beans and chocolate curls

To make the pastry: Sift the flour into a bowl, add the butter, and rub it in finely. Stir in the walnuts, sugar, and egg and mix to a firm dough.

Knead the dough until it is smooth. Roll it out thinly and use to line a 9-inch round loose-bottomed tart pan. Chill 30 minutes.

Preheat the oven to 400°F.

Bake the pastry shell "blind" until lightly browned at the edges, 15–20 minutes.

While the shell is baking make the filling: Place the milk, chocolate, butter, and coffee in a pan and heat gently until the chocolate has melted. Blend the cornstarch, egg yolks, and liqueur together, add this to the pan, and bring to a boil, stirring. Simmer 1 minute. Off the heat, stir in the cream and pour into the pastry shell. Leave until cold.

Pipe the whipped cream over the tart and decorate with chocolate-coated coffee beans and curls.

PECAN-CHOCOLATE TART

SERVES 8

FOR THE PASTRY

1⅓ cups flour

½ tsp baking powder

10 tbsp butter or margarine, cut into small pieces

5 tbsp sugar

grated zest of 1 washed lime

1 egg

FOR THE FILLING

¾ cup sugar

6 tbsp butter or margarine, softened

2 eggs, beaten

1 tbsp cornstarch

2 cups ground pecans

3 oz semisweet chocolate, chopped into small pieces

2 tbsp chocolate liqueur

FOR DECORATION

pecan halves

To make the pastry: Sift the flour and baking powder into a bowl, add the butter or margarine, and rub it in finely with your fingertips. Stir in the sugar, lime zest and egg and mix to a firm dough.

Knead the dough until it is smooth. Roll it out thinly and use to line a 10-inch round tart or quiche dish, reserving the trimmings. Chill 30 minutes.

Preheat the oven to 375°F.

To make the filling: Place the sugar and butter or margarine in a bowl and beat until light and fluffy. Add the eggs a little at a time, beating well after each addition. Fold in the cornstarch, ground pecans, chocolate, and chocolate liqueur until evenly blended.

Pour the mixture into the pastry shell. Use the pastry trimmings to make a lattice across the top. Bake until the filling has set, 40–50 minutes.

Decorate with pecan halves and serve warm or cold, cut in wedges.

For RHUBARB AND GINGER CREAM TART *use thin, young hothouse rhubarb, available early in the season. Field-grown rhubarb, with thick, deep-red stalks and a very tart flavor, is much coarser than the early variety.* STEM GINGER, *preserved in syrup or candied, is available in Asian markets and many supermarkets.*

CRÈME BRÛLÉE TARTLETS

MAKES 4

FOR THE PASTRY
1¼ cups flour
1 stick butter or margarine, cut into small pieces
5 tbsp sugar
1 egg white
FOR THE FILLING
½ cup raspberries
½ cup wild strawberries
2 eggs + 2 extra yolks
1 tbsp sugar
1¼ cups light cream
FOR THE TOPPING
¼ cup packed light brown sugar
wild strawberries

To make the pastry: Sift the flour into a bowl, add the butter or margarine, and rub it in finely with your fingertips. Stir in the sugar and egg white and mix together with a fork to form a firm dough.

Knead the dough until it is smooth. Roll it out thinly and use to line four 4½-inch loose-bottomed fluted tartlet molds. Chill 30 minutes.

Preheat the oven to 400°F. Bake the pastry shells "blind" until lightly browned at the edges, 10–15 minutes. Reduce the oven temperature to 325°F.

Arrange the fruit in the pastry shells. Place the eggs, egg yolks, and sugar in a bowl and whisk until smooth. Bring the cream just to a boil in a small saucepan and pour it onto the eggs, whisking all the time. Strain the custard into the pastry shells. Bake until the custard has set, 25–30 minutes. Let cool.

Just before serving, make the topping: Preheat the broiler. Sprinkle the brown sugar over the surface of the custard. Place the tartlets under the broiler to caramelize the sugar, about 1 minute. Let cool, then remove the tartlets from their molds, and decorate with wild strawberries.

RHUBARB AND GINGER CREAM TART

SERVES 6

FOR THE PASTRY
1¼ cups flour
1½ tsp ground ginger
6 tbsp butter, cut into small pieces
3–4 tbsp syrup from preserved stem ginger
FOR THE FILLING
⅔ cup sugar
¾ lb hothouse rhubarb, cut into 1-inch lengths
2 pieces of preserved stem ginger, sliced
2 eggs, separated
¼ cup whipping cream
FOR DECORATION
confectioners' sugar

Make the pastry: Sift the flour and ground ginger into a bowl, add the butter, and rub it in finely. Stir in the ginger syrup and mix to a firm dough.

Knead until smooth. Roll it out thinly and use to line a 9-inch round loose-bottomed fluted tart pan. Chill 30 minutes. Preheat the oven to 400°F.

Bake the pastry shell "blind" 10–15 minutes.

While the shell is baking make the filling: Place half the sugar in a pan with 1 tablespoon of water. Bring to a boil, stirring until the sugar has dissolved. Add the rhubarb and cook, shaking occasionally, until barely tender, 2–3 minutes. Drain, reserving the juices, and arrange it with the ginger in the shell. Whisk the egg yolks, remaining sugar, and cream in a bowl until thick. Stir in the juices.

Beat the egg whites until stiff. Fold into the cream mixture. Pour into the shell and bake until just set, 30–40 minutes. Dust thickly with confectioners' sugar and serve hot or cold.

Left: Rhubarb and Ginger Cream Tart; right Crème Brûlée Tartlets

PINE NUTS, also known as piñon nuts, pignoli, and Indian nuts, are the small creamy-colored fruits of the stone pine, which grows in the sandy areas of the Mediterranean, in Mexico, and in the Southwest United States. The nuts are found at the base of the scales that form the pine cones. Buy the nuts in small quantities as their oil content is high and they turn rancid rapidly.

PINE NUT TART

SERVES 8

FOR THE PASTRY
¾ cup whole wheat flour
½ cup + 2 tbsp all-purpose flour, sifted
6 tbsp butter or margarine, cut into small pieces
2 tbsp light brown sugar
3–4 tbsp sour cream
FOR THE FILLING
1 stick butter or margarine
½ cup packed light brown sugar
1⅓ cups ground almonds
1 tbsp rice flour
2 tbsp Madeira wine
2 eggs
1½ cups pine nuts
1 tbsp honey, warmed

To make the pastry: Mix the flours in a bowl, add the butter or margarine, and rub it in finely with your fingertips. Stir in the sugar and sour cream and mix together with a fork to form a firm dough.

Knead the dough until it is smooth. Roll it out thinly and use to line an 8-inch square loose-bottomed fluted tart pan. Chill 30 minutes.

Preheat the oven to 350°F.

To make the filling: Place the butter or margarine and sugar in a bowl and beat until light and fluffy, 2–3 minutes. Add the ground almonds, rice flour, Madeira, and eggs and mix together until evenly blended. Beat until smooth and glossy. Stir in 1¼ cups of the pine nuts.

Put the nut filling in the pastry shell, spread it evenly, and smooth the top. Sprinkle with the remaining pine nuts. Bake until well risen and golden brown, 60–65 minutes.

Let cool in the pan, then unmold carefully. Brush the top with the warmed honey and serve warm or cold, cut into 8 pieces.

SOUR CREAM AND RAISIN TART

SERVES 6

FOR THE PASTRY
1¼ cups flour
6 tbsp butter or margarine, cut into small pieces
5 tbsp sugar
3 tbsp sour cream
FOR THE FILLING
1⅓ cups raisins
7 tbsp sugar
1 tbsp flour
1 tsp apple-pie spice
2 tsp grated zest from a washed lemon
⅔ cup sour cream
2 eggs, beaten

To make the pastry: Sift the flour into a bowl, add the butter or margarine, and rub it in finely with your fingertips. Stir in the sugar and sour cream and mix with a fork to form a firm dough.

Knead the dough until it is smooth. Roll it out thinly and use to line an 8-inch round loose-bottomed fluted tart pan, reserving the pastry trimmings for decoration. Chill 30 minutes.

Preheat the oven to 375°F.

To make the filling: Place the raisins in a saucepan with ⅔ cup water. Bring to a boil, cover, and simmer until tender, 3–4 minutes. Stir in the sugar, flour, spice, and lemon zest and cook 1 minute, stirring. Let cool.

In a bowl beat together the sour cream and eggs. Add the raisin mixture and stir until well blended. Pour the mixture into the pastry shell. Roll out the pastry trimmings and cut into thin strips. Decorate the tart with a lattice of pastry strips.

Bake until the filling has risen and is golden brown, 45–50 minutes. Let cool in the pan, then unmold carefully. Serve in wedges.

ORANGE RICE TART

SERVES 12

FOR THE PASTRY

1⅓ cups flour
1 stick butter or margarine, cut into small pieces
5 tbsp sugar
2 tsp grated zest from a washed orange
1 egg, beaten

FOR THE FILLING

⅓ cup arborio or other short-grain rice
1½ cups milk
2 tbsp orange flower water
1 fresh bay leaf
1 stick butter
7 tbsp sugar
2 eggs, separated
¼ cup apricot preserves
2 oranges, peeled and cut into sections

FOR DECORATION

1 washed orange, thinly sliced

To make the pastry: Sift the flour into a bowl, add the butter or margarine, and rub it in finely with your fingertips. Stir in the sugar, orange zest, and egg and mix together to a firm dough.

Knead the dough on a lightly floured surface until it is smooth. Roll it out thinly and use to line an 11-×8-inch rectangular loose-bottomed tart pan or form set on a baking sheet. Chill 1 hour.

To make the filling: Place the rice, milk, orange flower water, and bay leaf in a saucepan. Bring to a boil, stirring occasionally. Then cover and cook over very low heat until the rice has absorbed the milk and is soft and sticky, 30–35 minutes. Set the pan in cold water to cool it quickly. Discard the bay leaf. Preheat the oven to 350°F.

Beat the butter, half the sugar, and the egg yolks together in a bowl. Add the rice and blend well.

Beat the egg whites until stiff. Add the remaining sugar a little at a time, beating well after each addition, until stiff again. Fold this gently into the rice mixture until evenly blended.

Spread the apricot preserves over the bottom of the pastry shell and cover this with the orange sections. Top with the rice meringue filling, spreading to cover smoothly. Bake until the pastry is pale golden and the filling has set, 75–85 minutes.

Let cool, then unmold carefully. Serve warm or cold decorated with the orange slices.

Pine Nut Tart

ITALIAN CHEESE TART

SERVES 6

FOR THE PASTRY
¾ cup flour
6 tbsp butter or margarine, cut into small pieces
2 tbsp sugar
grated zest of 1 washed lemon
1 egg white
FOR THE FILLING
⅓ cup chopped candied fruits
1 oz semisweet chocolate, chopped into small pieces
2½ tbsp raisins
1 tbsp Marsala wine
1 cup ricotta or cream cheese
2 tbsp sugar
1 egg, separated, + 1 extra yolk

To make the pastry: Sift the flour into a bowl, add the butter or margarine, and rub it in finely with your fingertips. Stir in the sugar, lemon zest, and egg white and mix to a firm dough.

Knead the dough until it is smooth. Roll it out thinly and use to line a 7-inch round loose-bottomed flutted tart pan. Chill 30 minutes.

Preheat the oven to 400°F.

Bake the pastry shell "blind" until lightly browned at the edges, 10–15 minutes. Reduce the oven temperature to 350°F.

While the shell is baking make the filling: Place the candied fruits, chocolate, raisins, and Marsala in a bowl and stir well to mix.

Place the cheese in another bowl. Add the sugar and egg yolks and beat well. Beat the egg white in a third bowl until stiff. Fold this into the cheese mixture, together with the mixed fruits. Spread the filling in the pastry shell.

Bake in the cooler oven until the filling has set and the pastry is golden brown, 45–50 minutes. Let cool in the pan.

RICOTTA is a white and creamy cheese with a soft, slightly granular texture. It has a bland sweetish flavor and can be eaten fresh with fruit or used for cheesecake and pastries and in savory dishes, especially with pasta.

BELGIAN TART

SERVES 6

FOR THE PASTRY
½ cup cream cheese
4 tbsp butter, softened
1⅓ cups flour
3½ tbsp cornstarch
2 tbsp sugar
FOR THE FILLING
2 tbsp shredded coconut
2 tbsp light brown sugar
3 tbsp apricot preserves
2 nectarines, sliced
FOR DECORATION
strips of fresh coconut
nectarine slices

To make the pastry: Place the cream cheese and butter in a bowl and beat until smooth. Stir in 2 tablespoons of water, the flour, cornstarch, and sugar and mix with a fork to form a firm dough.

Knead the dough on a lightly floured surface until it is smooth. Roll out two-thirds thinly and use to line an 8-inch round loose-bottomed fluted tart pan. Chill 30 minutes.

Preheat the oven to 400°F.

Make the filling: Shred the remaining dough and trimmings on a coarse grater. Mix together the coconut and sugar in a bowl.

Spread the apricot preserves over the bottom of the pastry shell and cover with the sliced nectarines. Top with the grated pastry dough and sprinkle with the coconut mixture.

Bake until lightly browned, 35–40 minutes. Serve warm or cold, decorated with strips of coconut and slices of nectarine.

Left: Belgian Tart; right: Orange Rice Tart (page 61)

INDEX

ACKNOWLEDGMENTS
The author would like to thank Mavis Giles for typing her copy at all hours, Michelle for her wonderful work on the photography, and Sue Storey and Mary Evans for their support.